Living Through History

THE RUSSIAN REVOLUTION

ELIZABETH CAMPLING

Batsford Academic and Educational
London

CONTENTS

THE RUSSIAN REVOLUTION   3

THE MEN OF ACTION:
Semen Kanatchikov   11
Alexander Shlyapnikov   14
Nikolai Sukhanov   18
Vladimir Korostovetz   21
Alexander Lukomsky   25
LIFE IN REVOLUTIONARY RUSSIA:
Louise Bryant   31
Arthur Ransome   34
Olga Chernov   37
Frank McCullagh   41
THE IMPACT ABROAD:
David Francis   47
Major H.N.H. Williamson   49
George Lansbury   53
Emma Goldman   56
THE AFTERMATH:
Elisaveta Fen   62
Lenin's Last Years   65

NOTES ON RUSSIAN POLITICS   68
DATE LIST   69
BOOK LIST   71
INDEX   72

Typeset by Tek-Art Ltd, West Wickham, Kent
Printed in Great Britain by
R.J. Acford
Chichester, Sussex
for the publishers
Batsford Academic and Educational,
an imprint of B.T. Batsford Ltd,
4 Fitzhardinge Street
London W1H 0AH

ISBN 0 7134 4671 4

ACKNOWLEDGMENTS

The Author and Publishers thank the following for
their kind permission to reproduce copyright
illustrations: BBC Hulton Picture Library, figures
14, 15, 29, 40, 43, 46, 47; Collection Viollet,
figures 18, 39; Mandel Archive, figures 16, 26, 27;
the Mansell Collection Ltd, figures 9, 12, 13, 19,
28, 30, 31, 32, 38, 42; Novosti Press Agency,
figures 2, 3, 4, 5, 7, 8, 10, 11, 17, 21, 22, 23, 24, 25,
34, 35, 36, 37, 41, 45; Photo Harlingue-Viollet,
figure 6; Popperfoto, figures 33, 34. The pictures
were researched by Patricia Mandel. Figures 1, 20
and 48 were drawn by R.F. Brien.
Cover pictures
The colour picture on the front cover is reproduced
by permission of Novosti Press Agency; the
portrait of Lukomsky is from the Mandel Archive;
the right-hand picture, from an engraving of
plundering a country house, is from the Mansell
Collection.

THE RUSSIAN REVOLUTION

The overthrow of the Tsarist regime in March 1917 was greeted with great enthusiasm by democrats and socialists everywhere. In his declaration of war against Germany a month later, the US President Wilson referred specifically to "the wonderful and heartening things that have been happening in the last few weeks in Russia". Eight months later the world was shaken by the news that a handful of hitherto disregarded revolutionaries had seized control of Russia's major cities and announced the birth of the Soviet Union, the world's first Communist state.

Three years of bloody civil war were to ensue before Bolshevik rule was finally established over the whole country in 1921, and by that time Soviet Russia was condemned and ostracized by her former allies, Britain, France and the United States,

2 Mutinies in the armed forces played a vital role in the overthrow of the Tsar. Here a detachment joins the February Revolution on Petrograd's Liteiny Prospect.

1

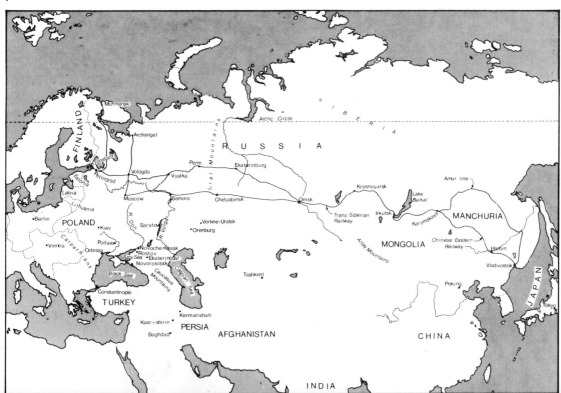

and had also proved a profound disappointment to many socialists. The philosopher, Bertrand Russell, returned from a brief visit in 1920 to write *The Theory and Practice of Bolshevism,* in which he concluded that:

while some forms of socialism are immeasurably better than capitalism, others are even worse. Among those that are worse I reckon the form that is being achieved in Russia.

Even among the Bolshevik leadership itself a faction had appeared – the Workers' Opposition – which accused the Party of having deviated from its ideal of "proletarian democracy". And before his death in 1924, Lenin himself was to express grave disquiet about the way in which Soviet politics were developing.

A partial explanation for this state of affairs lay in the peculiar conditions in which the revolution took place. The "February Rising" started as a spontaneous eruption of accumulated discontents. On the day that disorders first broke out in Petrograd, an agent of the Okhrana, the Tsarist secret police, reported:

The movement that has started has flared up without any party preparing it and without any preliminary discussion of a plan of action.

The pace of events in these early stages was dictated by the workers on the streets, the demoralized soldiers at the front, the mutinous sailors of Kronstadt and the land-hungry peasants. Any group that wished to assume leadership of the revolution would first have to harness to their own ends the energy and passion of the masses.

In 1917 it was the Bolsheviks under Lenin's leadership, abandoning orthodox Marxism and making shrewd tactical promises to a wide range of discontented groups, who proved the most adept politicians. While others pleaded with the workers to restrain their economic demands in the long-term interests of the revolution, Lenin's followers encouraged strikes and factory seizures; when the

Provisional Government postponed settlement of the land question until elections had been held for the Constituent Assembly, the Bolsheviks were quick to realize the political advantage this brought them. In the words of historian William H. Chamberlin:

In almost any other country a government menaced by extremist revolutionaries could turn for support to the propertied peasant or farmer class. There was obviously no support for the Provisional Government in the Russian villages during September and October 1917. And it was not the least sign of Lenin's genius as a revolutionary leader that he sensed the mood of the peasantry and the force and reality behind the agrarian revolution . . . the mobs of enraged villagers, who cared little whether the country was governed by Bolsheviki or Socialist Revolutionaries; but who were determined to burn out the neighbouring pomyschik [landlord] at any cost. (W.H. Chamberlin, *The Russian Revolution,* Grosset and Dunlop, New York, 1965)

In November 1917, on a wave of working-class enthusiasm and peasant indifference to the fate of the outgoing government, the Bolsheviks swept into power with almost ludicrous ease, the great city of Petrograd being captured by no more than twenty thousand poorly-trained Red Guard (the Bolsheviks' private army of sailors and industrial workers). Sixteen and a half million peasants, who had voted for the Socialist Revolutionary Party but who had been won over to the Bolshevik regime by the land nationalization decree of 8 November, raised not a voice in protest as the Constituent Assembly, Russia's first democratically-elected assembly, was disbanded by an armed minority.

If the Bolsheviks were to hold the power they had won so easily, however, the slogans of 1917, encouraging anarchy and destruction, would not suffice, for, as 1917 gave way to 1918, opposition to Bolshevik rule developed in many areas of Russia. (Historians have coined the blanket term "Whites" to describe the anti-Communist camp, although, in fact, the Whites never created a co-ordinated front and encompassed many shades of political opinion. Their opponents, on the other hand, proudly designated themselves the "Reds" – the traditional colour of international socialism – and the army they created in February 1918 is known today throughout the world as the "Red Army".) Workers' control and democratization gave way to war Communism and the restoration of traditional army discipline. Improvements in the standard of living were postponed to some indefinite point in the future. The urban proletariat responded with an unswerving loyalty that survived even the appalling privations of 1919-21, and the solid Communist allegiance of the big cities was never better demonstrated than in the defence of Petrograd against the Yudenitch offensive in October 1919. Trotsky recalled with pride:

3 This barricade erected on a major thoroughfare was one of the weapons used by the citizens of Petrograd to defend the city against Yudenitch's army in October 1919.

Everyone expected an early surrender of the city. . . . But as soon as the masses began to feel that Petrograd was not to be surrendered, and if necessary would be defended from within, in the streets and squares, the spirit changed at once. The more courageous and self-sacrificing lifted up their heads. Detachments of men and women, with trenching tools on their shoulders, filed out of the mills and factories . . .

The eyes of the women burned with especial fervour. . . . Not a few of them eventually armed themselves with rifles or took their places at the machine-guns. The whole city was divided into sections, controlled by staffs of workers . . . canals, gardens, walls and houses were fortified. . . . The whole southern part of the city was transformed into a fortress. Barricades were raised on many of the streets and squares. A new spirit was breathing from the workers' districts to the barracks, the rear units and even to the army in the field. (Leon Trotsky, *My Life*, Pelican, 1971)

Only when Bolshevik rule was finally secure did the frustrations and disappointments of unfulfilled expectations reveal themselves in the disturbances of 1921.

In his history of the Russian Revolution,

published in 1932, Trotsky wrote: "In the unstable poise of a scale only a small weight is needed to decide." If one reason were singled out that would explain the ultimate Bolshevik triumph, it would surely be the sense of class solidarity and faith in the future, which the Whites, for all their courageous and dedicated individuals, could never match.

The cities alone, however, could not win the civil war for the Bolsheviks. To supply and man the Red Army, peasant cooperation was essential; and the three or four thousand former army officers, who formed the core of the White regimes, were likewise dependent on their rural bases. The peasantry, war-weary, distrustful of all forms of strong government and wanting only to enjoy the land they had so recently acquired, fought willingly for neither side. In desperation, Red and White regimes alike resorted to requisitioning, conscription and forced labour, and created a peasant backlash that hit out at both indiscriminately. In the spring of 1919 the Bolsheviks were driven out of the Ukraine by peasants who had welcomed them as liberators three months before, only to see the area fall into the hands of Denikin's White armies. In turn, the White advance on Moscow was crippled as marauding bands of

4 Makhno (on the right, in a white hat) among a delegation of peasants visiting the Bolshevik Headquarters at Smolny in 1917. He rapidly became disillusioned with the new regime.

peasants, the "Green Guards", wrought havoc in their rear. Nestor Makhno, the most renowned of the Green commanders, explained their motives with a clarity few of his uneducated followers could have matched:

Any state destroys, suppresses, enslaves all the best innate spiritual values that push for freedom. . . . The Makhno movement reflects the striving of the lowest layers of the people for their self-emancipation and stands steadfastly for the defence of the toilers against the violence of white landlords and red commissars. (Quoted in M. Malet, *Nestor Makhno in the Russian Civil War*, London, 1982)

There were those in Russia who hoped to create out of peasant anarchism a third force, a democratic alternative to Red or White dictatorship. This dream proved illusory. At critical junctures during the civil war Green violence might tip the balance between contending factions, but it was too ill-organized and sporadic to be harnessed for constructive ends. Attempts by Socialist Revolutionaries to establish popular, anti-Bolshevik regimes at Samara and Archangel,

areas that had not yet experienced the full rigours of Soviet rule, failed to attract significant local support and fell under the control of a handful of determined White officers. Some years later a Samara politician, Klimushkin, came close to admitting the futility of his efforts:

We sent our friends to the villages to organise the peasants. The work, though steadily progressing, was very slow and it was always clear that without some external stimulus no hope . . . could be entertained in the near future.

The peasant guerillas of Siberia and the Ukraine, who brought Kolchak and Denikin to ruin, did not then band together against the new tyranny of the Red Army but spent themselves in ill-organized, unco-ordinated and futile acts of rebellion, Makhno himself fighting on until he was driven into Rumania in 1922. In such an environment, the views of a minority were likely to prevail and the emergence of permanent dictatorship was a constant danger.

Petrograd
From 1703 until 1918 the capital of Russia was the city of St Petersburg on the River Neva. In August 1914, in a spirit of xenophobia, the name was Russianized to Petrograd, the name by which the city was known throughout the revolutionary period. Where contemporaries still used the old name, this has been left unchanged in the text, and the city may therefore appear under either title. In 1918 the status of capital was transferred to Moscow, and in 1924, in honour of Lenin, Petrograd's name was changed to Leningrad, the name by which the city is still known today.

Dating of Russian Events
In 1917 Russia still used the Julian calendar, which had long since been abandoned elsewhere, and Russian dates in this period run thirteen days behind those used in the rest of Europe. The Communist government brought Russia into line with the West in 1918. To avoid confusion, the dating used throughout this book has been standardized and the modern calendar used. The first revolution, therefore, began on 8 March, not 23 February; the Bolshevik coup took place on the night of 7/8 November, not 25/26 October. However, because the terms "February Revolution" and "October Revolution" were so widely used by contemporaries, these have been retained.

THE MEN OF ACTION

For the liberals of the first Provisional Government, supporters of constitutional rule and the rights of property, the main priorities of the February Revolution were to establish civil liberties and prepare for Russia's first-ever truly democratic elections. However, continued involvement in the Great War and the postponement of pressing social reforms until the election of a Constituent Assembly meant that such a government had little to offer the masses in the way of an immediate improvement in living and working conditions, and it won consistent support only from a politically ineffective section of the middle class.

Much more surprising was the ineffectiveness of the democratic socialists, who dominated the powerful Petrograd Soviet at the beginning of 1917. Both Mensheviks and Socialist Revolutionaries wanted to postpone the development of the revolution into a second, and more radical, phase until this could be achieved with the clear consent of the bulk of the working population, and with this cautious policy they squandered public support.

The Socialist Revolutionary Party, founded in 1902, believed that the assassination of key government personalities would trigger off the overthrow of the Tsarist autocracy, and that out of the ensuing chaos the peasant majority would construct a socialist system based on the common ownership of land. It was they who had been responsible for the assassination of the Grand Duke Sergei, uncle of the Tsar and Governor-General of Moscow, in 1905. After the February Revolution, however, they adopted a cautious policy, postponing radical land reform until such a change would be authorized by a freely-elected Constituent Assembly. Thus they lost the allegiance of the peasantry to the Bolsheviks.

The Mensheviks (one wing of the Russian Marxist Party, which split in 1903 into two factions, the Bolsheviks and Mensheviks) remained strict adherents to orthodox Marxism. They maintained that the dream of a workers' government must be postponed until some far distant day when the urban proletariat (industrial working class) would be politically mature enough to run their own affairs. For the soviets to seize power immediately would be a grievous mistake. An editorial in a Menshevik newspaper in March 1917 spelt out their version of the situation:

The Provisional Government is the government of the revolution and corresponds to the revolutionary level at which revolutionary Russia now stands. Our task is to aid it in bringing the revolution to its completion, and at the same time to hinder any attempts on its part to retard or turn back this revolution. But this second task will also be best achieved not . . . by attempts at seizure of power by the proletariat, but by an organised pressure on the government and by an indefatigable propagation of our views among the backward sections of the population. (Quoted in Kerensky and Browder, ed., *The Russian Provisional Government 1917*, Vol. I, Stamford University Press, 1961)

From then on the Mensheviks proceeded to commit political suicide by a doctrinaire insistence on an abstract Marxism that offered little more to the masses than did the moralizing of the liberals. This can be clearly seen in the debate over Russia's continued participation in the war. To fight, as had the Tsarist government, for territorial aggrandisement, was unthinkable; but for Russia to withdraw unilaterally would be a betrayal of the German workers, who hoped that the wartime hardships suffered by their people would hasten the coming of the German socialist revolution. If, however, the Mensheviks persuaded themselves, Tsarist war aims could be replaced by a declaration that the Allies were fighting for a just peace and the right of all peoples to self-determination, then the masses would see that "the government's policy was being conducted in correspondence with their own aspirations" (Tseretelli, a Georgian Menshevik) and their enthusiasm for the war would be renewed. To the war-weary troops, longing only to go home and join in the scramble for land, such distinctions meant little, but the Mensheviks lived on their illusions and Russia fought on. Every passing month found the democratic socialists more out of touch with popular feeling and the masses even more vulnerable to Lenin's simple promise that Bolshevism meant peace.

In these circumstances, the appointment of Mensheviks and Socialist Revolutionaries to the government in May 1917 and the appointment of Kerensky as Prime Minister in July did little to stem the Provisional Government's rising unpopularity and may even have hastened its downfall. Not least among the reasons for the ease of the Bolshevik takeover was the paralysis among socialist ministers faced with the bankruptcy of their political philosophy.

The civil war presented democratic socialists with an agonizing choice. Some, like the politicians at Archangel and Samara, persisted in the naive belief that a spontaneous popular uprising was about to break out against Reds and Whites alike. Others, like Martov, were doomed to a life of miserable inactivity, for they were convinced that the overthrow of the hated Bolsheviks would only thrust Russia into the arms of a White tyranny more dreadful than the Red. A third group was more realistic, accepted pragmatically that, for the time being, the only feasible choice lay between Red and White dictatorship, and took sides. His experience at Samara convinced Menshevik Ivan Maisky that "democracy has no future in Russia". He joined the Bolshevik Party and went on to serve as Soviet Ambassador to Britain between 1932 and 1943. When Maxim Gorky's newspaper, *Novaya Zhizn* (*New Life*), through whose pages he had tried to mitigate the harshness of Bolshevik rule, was closed

down, he concluded that he could best serve the cause of socialism by co-operating with the regime. Thereafter, he used his literary reputation and personal friendship with Lenin to protect artists and academics from the worst rigours of rationing, requisitioning and arbitrary arrest.

That the names of the Bolshevik leaders, particularly Lenin and Trotsky, are now among the best-known in modern history should not obscure the fact that in March 1917 they were but a band of exiles, whose influence on events in Russia was minimal. The party apparatus inside Russia itself, run primarily by recruits from the working class who combined daily work at the factory with illegal political activity, was still only rudimentary, and Bolshevism was the least popular form of socialism among the masses. This was confirmed by no less a witness than Alexander Shlyapnikov, who had been in charge of the day-to-day running of party affairs since 1914. Only at the naval base of Kronstadt could Bolshevism count on mass support before 1917.

The Bolsheviks were heretics, whose philosophy contravened the tenets of orthodox Marxism. If the Russian proletariat could seize power directly from the autocracy, argued their leader, Lenin, the slow Marxist route to socialism could be by-passed and a dictatorship of the proletariat be established forthwith. To galvanize support for such a coup, the masses were promised that Bolshevik rule would mean an immediate end to war and famine, the transfer of land to the peasants and a revolutionary system of democratic control in factory, army and government by popularly-elected soviets. Such unscrupulous promises shocked the democratic socialists, whose grasp of political reality was weaker than Lenin's, and there were even those among the Bolshevik leadership who had last-minute doubts about the wisdom of this course. At the secret meeting of 23 October 1917, at which plans for a Bolshevik insurrection were finalized, Kamenev and Zinoviev argued that the bulk of the Russian people had taken Bolshevik promises at face-value and were far from ready

5 A demonstration by soldiers, sailors and workers against the Provisional Government. When the Bolsheviks adopted the popular slogan "All Power to the Soviets", their influence amongst the masses rapidly increased.

for the sacrifices that would have to be made to consolidate Communist rule; to maintain power, therefore, the Bolsheviks might well have to impose an iron dictatorship that would not easily be lifted. History may well have proved them right, but in the short-term Lenin's tactics were brilliantly successful.

In the course of eight months between March and October 1917, this small band of fanatics created a disciplined political movement that was to hold the large cities loyal to Communism and provide a steadying force for the reluctant peasant levies of the Red Army. In a speech in December 1918 Trotsky, who had once disagreed with Lenin but who had finally joined the Bolshevik Party on his return from exile in the United States in May 1917, outlined the role of the dedicated Communist:

A soldier who is a party member has just the same rights as any other soldier – but not a hair's breadth more. He has only incomparably more duties. . . . Give me 3,000 deserters. Call them a regiment. I will find them a fighting regimental commander, a good commissar, fit officers for

the batallions, and these 3,000 deserters, in the course of four weeks in our revolutionary country, will produce a splendid regiment.

That there were many who lived up to this ideal was shown by the existence of an active Bolshevik fifth column in areas occupied by the Whites.

There were those, of course, especially among army officers and officials of the old regime, who distrusted the revolution from the start. In the atmosphere of 1917 they were doomed to ineffectualness, as was dramatically highlighted when railway workers sabotaged an attempt by conservative politicians to preserve the monarchy, and when the rank and file of the Cossack regiments refused to follow Kornilov. After 1917 such men formed the core of the White regimes and were joined by others, whose disillusionment with the revolution had developed more slowly. Not all came from the former ruling class; Denikin and Kolchak, for example, were the sons of peasants. Many, including the latter, regarded the restoration of the monarchy as neither desirable nor feasible. Yet most shared an insensitivity to the profound changes that had taken place in the social and political structure of Russia and displayed an inability to create a vision of the future that held any attraction for the peasantry or for the non-Russian nationalities. Denikin, for instance, was steadfastly determined that the frontiers of the old Tsarist Empire should remain intact, but this cherished belief in "Great Russia, whole and undivided" (speech to the Kuban Rada, traditional parliament of the Kuban Cossacks, November 1918) made effective cooperation with the Cossack atamans, on whose territories he was based, very difficult.

Moreover, the Whites never achieved that disciplined cohesion that became the hallmark of the Communist Party and stiffened the Red Army. Hodgson, a British journalist who accompanied Denikin's armies, chronicled numerous cases among White officers of drunkenness, profiteering and offensive behaviour towards civilians. While desertion was common in both camps, the demoralized

6 White artillery from General Wrangel's army, 1920. Contemporaries regarded Wrangel as the only senior White commander with qualities of leadership to rival those of Trotsky. When he succeeded General Denikin in March 1920, however, it was already too late to save the White armies of southern Russia from total defeat.

disintegration of the southern and Siberian armies in the early months of 1920 has no equivalent in the annals of the Red Army. There is no simple explanation for this difference. That the White movements contained men of many diverse political opinions, united only in their hatred of Communism and without a common philosophy, played a part; so too did the indifferent quality of the White leadership. It is ironic that a Marxist party, for whom impersonal economic and social forces were more important in shaping history than the actions of individuals, should owe its greatest triumph to the quality of its leaders, for no White general ever matched the political acumen of Lenin or the charisma of Trotsky. Denikin's memoirs, for example, reflect a bewildered man with little control over the forces he led, and a quotation from them is, perhaps, a fitting epitaph. Even at the height of White fortunes:

The troops of the army of the South did not avoid the general malady and they blotted their reputation by pogroms against the Jews. . . . The inner sores festered in the atmosphere of hatred. The pogroms brought suffering to the Russian people, but they also affected the morale of the troops, warped their minds and destroyed discipline. (A. Denikin, *The Russian Turmoil*, London, 1922)

The spectacular success of the Bolshevik Party in 1917 owed much to the dedication of humble Party workers, who kept the Party alive in Russia during the dark days of Tsarist repression, when political activity was illegal and the leadership in exile. The identity of many remains obscure, but Semen Kanatchikov, destined to become a high-ranking Soviet official, has left a first-hand account of the experiences that turned an illiterate peasant into a hardened revolutionary conspirator.

Semen Kanatchikov (1879-1940)

There is little to distinguish the early life of "Senka" Kanatchikov, born in the village of Gusevo near Moscow, from that of millions of other peasants. His father, Ivan, drank heavily and was often violent towards his wife and children. The religious observances of the Orthodox Church were strictly enforced and the Kanatchikov offspring lived in fear of the torments of hell. Surrounded by ignorance and hardship, only four of Senka's twelve brothers and sisters survived into adulthood.

Neither was his departure, at the age of sixteen, for the industries of Moscow particularly remarkable. His older brother had already been forced to supplement the family income by spending the winter months in a factory, and the despotic Ivan assumed that Senka's absence would likewise be temporary – a prelude to his marriage to a country girl and his adoption of the traditional farmer's life. Korovin, an old workman from Gusevo, was assigned to look after him and make sure that he attended church regularly.

Senka, however, developed other ideas. Within a year he had become a skilled pattern-maker, designing and preparing the moulds from which the machinery to modernize Russian industry would be made. In this period of rapid industrialization it was a vital and highly-regarded trade, and Reginald Zelnik, editor of Kanatchikov's memoirs, believes:

It was the successful striving for mastery over the unfamiliar technology of his new industrial world that enabled him, in the course of the next two years, to draw the inner strength and

7 Workers from Petrograd's Putilov Factory at home, around the turn of the century. It was in conditions like these that revolution was bred.

8 A factory in Tsarist Russia. In the rapidly-expanding industries, socialism won many recruits.

confidence to turn his back on his village and, in defiance of his father's wishes, begin to think of himself, with enormous pride, as a permanent worker. (R. Zelnik, "An Introduction to the Memoirs of the Russian Workers, Semen Kanatchikov and Matvei Fisher", *Russian Review,* July/Oct. 1976)

Kanatchikov's first act of rebellion was to reject religion. Listening to the arguments of the atheist, Savinov, who worked next to him on the factory bench:

My beliefs, my views of the surrounding world, the moral foundations with which I had lived and grown up, so nicely, so peacefully, comfortably, suddenly began to shake. . . . Shivers ran up my spine, I became cold and terrified, as if I were preparing to leap across some abyss. But at the same time I felt high and free when I remembered that together with the old principles would also disappear that terrible nightmare that threatened me with the tortures of hell.

He left the apartment that he shared with Korovin and moved in with a like-minded comrade.

At Gusevo, during the Christmas holiday of 1896-7, the final break came. Rejecting the

bride chosen for him by his father, Kanatchikov spurned for ever the tedium of village life:

I was drawn unconsciously to the factory, to the people who worked there, who were becoming my own people, my relatives. I felt impassioned by the factory, by its stern poetry of labour, which was becoming dearer and closer to me than . . . the torpid village life.

Now he was a fully-fledged proletarian, Kanatchikov's attention turned towards the harsh conditions of the people among whom he had chosen to live. As a skilled worker he earned relatively high wages, but the hours were gruellingly long. An 11½-hour working day left him little energy for anything but sleep. When workers were granted three 8-hour days in honour of the coronation of Nicholas II in 1896, Kanatchikov was struck by the "sweetness" of the shorter working day. Savinov provided him with a stream of illegal publications analysing the plight of the urban worker. Writing over thirty years later, Senka recalled that one of the earliest Marxist pamphlets, Plekhanov's account of the labour movement in St Petersburg in the 1870s, had made a particular impact on him. He resolutely turned his back on the temptations of urban life that might distract him from the struggle for better living conditions. His father once confessed to a neighbour that he was amazed "at the kind of child I've sired; he drinks no vodka, smokes no tobacco, doesn't play cards". Senka decided never to marry, for:

To raise a family meant, at best, to add the suffering of their [the workers'] dear ones to their own, and at worst to abandon the revolution under the weight of family burdens.

Agitation on the shop-floor earned him the sack in 1898, and Zelnik concludes that by this stage "for Senka dismissal on these grounds was virtually a triumph and certainly no disgrace".

Although by now a confirmed militant, Kanatchikov was not as yet a member of any revolutionary organization, nor did he have a coherent political philosophy. In the autumn of 1898, however, he departed for St Petersburg in search of the "spirited comradely life" he believed he would find in the capital. He deliberately settled in the Neva Gate area of the city, a centre of working-class radicalism, and here he earned his first prison sentence, a ten-day stretch for beating up an abusive foreman. He also encountered, for the first time, the Social Democratic and the Socialist Revolutionary parties and their student adherents. For the uneducated Kanatchikov it was something new, something

exciting, interesting . . . it confronted me with a whole series of new questions and stimulated my thirst for knowledge. . . . [The students] seemed to me to be extraordinary people, who grasped all knowledge in their hands and had ready answers to all questions.

He steeped himself in revolutionary literature and became a Marxist, but his admiration for the intelligentsia was short-lived. They made him feel socially inadequate; he hated the way he and his fellow workers were paraded at meetings as genuine specimens of the "politically-conscious worker" and "any stupidity that we uttered in our confusion would be met with condescending approval". More significantly, he feared that the students treated revolutionary activities as an adolescent amusement that could always be abandoned when the going became tough. In exile in the Arctic in 1903, Kanatchikov noticed that middle-class deportees often received money and food parcels from relatives, something that working-class exiles had to do without.

From 1899 to 1905 Kanatchikov led a chequered career, serving two prison

9 Political prisoners of the Tsarist regime being led through the streets of Petrograd on the first stage of their journey to exile in Siberia.

sentences and two periods of internal exile for his political activities. In January 1905 he made a crucial decision to "choose a new speciality" and become "a professional revolutionary". He joined the Bolshevik Party, which at that time enjoyed little popularity among the working class, and adopted the code name "Egorov". Zelnik sees Kanatchikov's choice as a logical one, for:

Revolutionary dedication, the very quality Kanatchikov had seen lacking in the intelligentsia of the past, was the salient feature of these self-selected revolutionary professionals, men who – whatever their other defects or qualities – left no doubt that, like Kanatchikov, they had really "burned their bridges behind them".

For Kanatchikov the commitment was certainly life-long. In the early 1930s, by then a senior Soviet official, he paid tribute to the role the Party had played in his life. It had become, he wrote, his "family, hearth and home" and his "comrades in struggle" had taken the place of "brothers, sisters, father and mother".

Kanatchikov's memoirs end with the year 1905 and only a bare outline of the last thirty-five years of his life can be pieced together. Exiled to Siberia in 1911, he was released by the February Revolution and played an active role in Siberian soviets during the civil war. Thereafter he specialized in educational matters, becoming, in turn, Dean of the Communist University in Petrograd 1920-4, head of the party history section of the Central Committee 1925-6, and Tass correspondent in Czechoslovakia 1926-8. Of his feelings about the course of Soviet history after Lenin's death little can be deduced. He apparently co-operated with Stalin in the early years, for until 1934 his name appears on numerous official documents and the two volumes of his memoirs were published between 1929 and 1934. He died in 1940 at the age of sixty-one. Over the years in between, a blanket of silence lies.

Alexander Shlyapnikov (1883-c.1937)

The man who was perhaps most responsible for keeping the Bolshevik Party alive in Russia before 1917 was Alexander Shlyapnikov, one of the few prominent Bolsheviks whose origins were truly working-class and who never lost touch with his roots. Born in the village of Doshchatoe near Murom, on a tributary of the River Volga, where "men and women worked without a murmur, submissively bending their backs for paupers' wages whatever the length of the working day", he received only three years of elementary schooling, then trained in engineering workshops as a turner and fitter. His career as a revolutionary began with the reading of Marxist pamphlets illegally distributed on the shop-floor, and he joined the Bolshevik Party in 1903. Exiled as a dangerous radical in 1908, Shlyapnikov spent the next six years working in factories in Britain and France, returning to St Petersburg under an assumed name and with a false passport in the spring of 1914. He felt that he had come home in more senses than one:

I went round the working class districts, the plants and factories, the same old walls and hooters which involuntarily aroused memories of the heroic period of the Petersburg proletariat's struggle between 1900 and 1907. I was drawn towards my native bench, and wanted to submerge myself in those toothed, cranked

10 A workers' demonstration in the Lena goldfields, 1912. Experienced revolutionaries were well-aware that such incidents rarely seriously threatened the stability of the Tsarist regime.

noisy surroundings, so I decided to turn down an honourable and distinguished post as a party official "at the centre" and go to a plant. (*On the Eve of 1917,* London, 1982)

He found a job as a turner at the New Lessner works in the Vyborg suburb and settled down to a life of trade union organization and shop-floor agitation.

In September 1914 Shlyapnikov was summoned by the Party leadership to Stockholm and given the job of liaison officer between the leaders exiled in Switzerland and Scandinavia and the Party cells inside Russia itself. His duties included smuggling Party literature into Russia from abroad and creating an effective underground Party organization. For the next two and a half years Shlyapnikov led a risky and roving life, commuting illegally between Stockholm and Petrograd.

He had the satisfaction of watching discontent in Russia increase with every month of the war. The Petrograd he had left in 1914 had been filled with patriotic enthusiasm, even among the proletariat; he returned in August 1915 in time to participate in a rash of street demonstrations brought about by deteriorating living and working conditions. On 9 January 1916, 40,000 marched in protest against the government in the Vyborg district and the tram maintenance men struck. Most encouraging of all:

During the demonstrations workers met soldiers; a friendly exchange of greeting would then take place. At the sight of the red banner . . . the soldiers took off their caps and shouted "Hurrah!"

This soon became a common occurrence. When police tried to break up a demonstration outside the New Lessner works, where Shlyapnikov himself had once been employed:

soldiers from the neighbouring barracks who were looking over a low fence into the street knocked down the fence, beating up and driving out the police. Cossacks were called out to arrest the soldiers and workers. But the Cossacks decided not to act and they were withdrawn. The soldiers' behaviour caused consternation among the military hierarchy. . . . One hundred and thirty men were arrested and threatened with court-martial.

Shlyapnikov was also delighted to learn that

the miners of the Donets Basin, once the most tractable of workforces, had come out on strike and that Marxism was spreading rapidly among them.

Shlyapnikov was forced to admit, however, that these disturbances were more of an annoyance than a real threat to the Tsarist government. Unless individual working-class protests could be properly co-ordinated, there was no hope of real revolution. Unfortunately, the creation of a country-wide network of Bolshevik cells in factories and barracks moved frustratingly slowly. Constant police-surveillance meant that the average survival-time for an illegal Party worker in Petrograd was about three months. Shlyapnikov was absent from Russia between March and October 1916; on his return he found that:

The . . . party workers whom I had organised in the autumn of 1915 during my first wartime visit from abroad had all been knocked out of action. Several were in jail while others were in exile or expecting it. . . . The job . . . had to be started again from scratch.

Funds were perennially short. If a Party man were sent into the provinces, he could not be guaranteed even one month's financial support. Shlyapnikov himself once had to take a factory job merely "to put some order back into my clothing and to re-equip myself with underwear, which had got pretty tatty during my illegal travels". Poverty and police harassment made the printing of Party literature so difficult that all kinds of ingenious means had to be resorted to. On one occasion, Comrade Antipov, who worked for Altschuler's printing press,

picked twelve or thirteen determined and bold printers from each trade and on the night of 17 December they carried out an armed seizure of the print shop. Having gained control of the press, the printer comrades locked up the night-shift and . . . set up and rolled off several thousand copies of "Proletarskii Golos" ["Proletarian Voice"].

Okhrana agents planted in the Party were

11 The Baltic naval base of Kronstadt was an early hot-bed of Bolshevism. Here a trusted detachment of sailors check the identity of visitors to Smolny.

a constant danger and operations were often mysteriously betrayed. For months Shlyapnikov suspected Comrade Chernomazov of being a stooge, but he could never prove it to the satisfaction of other Party members. The strongest Party organization proved to be that set up at the naval base of Kronstadt, but even here Shlyapnikov considered that Party discipline was far from perfect and the sailors had developed a tendency to assume that "the navy could by itself, independently of the general struggle, lead to a victorious revolution".

The personal life of a Party worker was fraught with danger and discomfort. On one of his visits to Petrograd in the autumn of 1916 Shlyapnikov found himself under police surveillance. He decided, therefore, that:

settling down with my own flat, a valid passport and other such luxuries was in such a situation to court real disaster. To have any possibility of countering the stratagems of the agents I had to have as many lodgings as possible. Comrades helped me to find places, and I had a particular spot for each night. These were dispersed in various parts of Petersburg, including its extremities. . . . My life was turning into a perpetual wandering. It was hard to write, read and at times even to think, as often, when I was tired, hospitable comrades engaged to me with their political programmes and enjoyable conversation deep into the night. You could survive like that for two or three months but my physical energy did not allow more.

Shlyapnikov always felt uncomfortable when forced to work closely with intellectuals. When an argument over Marxist dogma blew up into a full-scale row among the Stockholm exiles, during which comrades cut each other dead in the street, he was furious, for:

Contacts with and work for Russia were the first to suffer, and these for me counted above all else. I had imagined that you could keep your opinion on this or that point of our programme and fight for its adoption, but I could not see the need for animosity and least of all for damaging the workers' cause itself with such animosity. This phenomenon is, however, endemic in our intelligentsia, which is so doctrinaire in defence of its "principles" that it will ever abandon the work in hand.

Shlyapnikov and Comrade Litvinov once went to the station to meet Bukharin (a member of the Party Central Committee and a close associate of Lenin) and his wife, who were arriving from Switzerland. Neither Russian knew the Bukharins by sight but had no doubt that they would recognize them among the crowd by their "wandering gazes and absent-minded expressions". That Bukharin never ceased to irritate Shlyapnikov beyond endurance is shown by the fact that in his memoirs, published in the Soviet Union in 1923, Shlyapnikov baldly referred to Bukharin – by then a prominent Soviet politician – as "the type of impractical Russian intellectual for whom I had to think out every detail".

Shlyapnikov was honest enough to admit that, for all his energy and dedication, the Russian end of Bolshevik Party organization consisted in early 1917 only of "little organizations, scattered around factories, plants and mines" which did not "at that stage have any military know-how at their disposal" and played next to no part in the February Revolution. In 1917 itself, however,

Shlyapnikov's organizational talents came into their own. Sukhanov (see pages 18-21), who met him frequently in the Soviet, dismissed him as "an experienced conspirator, a first-rate technical organizer and a practical trade-unionist", who "as a politician was quite incapable of grasping the essence of things" and "lacked all independence of thought". What the over-intellectual Menshevik failed to realize, however, was that the future lay not with those who agonized over the "correct" theoretical course of the revolution, but with those who acted on the opportunities of the moment. Shlyapnikov's contacts on the shop-floor and his understanding of working-class aspirations were to prove invaluable to Bolshevik success. He organized the Vyborg detachment of the Red Guard, was intimately involved in the planning of the November coup and became Commissar (minister) for Labour in the first Communist administration.

In 1921, however, Shlyapnikov found himself in rebellion against the Party leadership. As one of the founders of the Workers' Opposition, which advocated that control of industry should be taken away from the Party bureaucrats and handed back to the workers themselves, he was expelled from the

12 The November Revolution was carried out by an untrained army of Red Guard recruited among soldiers, sailors and urban workers. In this idealized drawing of a scene from 1917, Lenin and Stalin display their common touch.

Central Committee in 1922. Remaining true to his simple belief that a Communist government should put the interests of the proletariat first, he stood aloof from the power struggles of the 1920s, explaining in an article in *Pravda* that neither side had any real concern with the conditions of the working class. It *is* possible that his memoirs were intended as the first blow in a campaign against those he believed were betraying the spirit of the movement; in them he did not flinch from making derogatory references to powerful colleagues. In the effort to raise funds before 1917, for example, appeals had been made to wealthy sympathizers, but, Shlyapnikov recalled:

all our efforts to obtain financial support from former social democrats . . . suffered failure. I personally sent people out to see some of these gentlemen (who are today "comrades" and members of our Russian Communist Party) and sounded out the ground, but without success.

If such a campaign was intended, however, it did not materialize and we do not know why. Shlyapnikov made his peace with the Party leadership in 1926, abandoned politics for writing (he wrote a massive four-volume history of the year 1917) and was finally arrested in the purges of the 1930s. Unlike other "Old Bolsheviks", however, he did not appear in a show trial and simply disappeared from history. It is tempting to believe that he was too tough and independent-minded to be bullied into making a public confession to crimes he did not commit, but of this there is no real evidence.

Nikolai Sukhanov (1873-c.1931)

Nikolai Himmer was a member of that middle-class intelligentsia that provided Russia with so many of her revolutionary leaders. His revolutionary career began when, at the age of twenty-one, he joined the forerunner of the Socialist Revolutionary Party, eventually being imprisoned on a charge of running an underground printing shop. Released under the 1905 amnesty, he was converted to Marxism, left the Socialist Revolutionaries and did not formally join another political party until May 1917, when he joined Martov's splinter group, the Menshevik Internationalists. Between 1905 and 1917 he was closely involved in underground journalism, and it was during this period that he adopted the pseudonym "Sukhanov", by which he was known to the Okhrana and by which posterity remembers him. The February Revolution found him living an amusing double-life. He had been banished from St Petersburg in May 1914 but:

though under the sentence of banishment, I spent most of my time, up to the revolution itself, living underground in the capital – sometimes on a false passport, sometimes sleeping in a different place every night, sometimes slipping past the night-porter in the shadows . . . to my own flat, where my family was living. . . .

Moreover, my illegal position did not stop me from working as an economist, under my own name, in a government department, the Ministry of Agriculture, in a section that dealt with the irrigation of Turkestan. [*The Russian Revolution*, O.U.P., 1955]

As a non-party man, a self-designated "wild one", with numerous acquaintances among the revolutionary leadership, Sukhanov believed that he was in a unique position to influence events, and he has left the only full-length, eye-witness account of 1917. The seven hundred pages of memoirs are a chronicle of nine months of frenzied activity, for during this period Sukhanov rarely slept at home, spoke in all the important debates in the Petrograd Soviet, acted as liaison officer between the Soviet and the Provisional Government in the early weeks, was an intimate spectator at crucial events including Lenin's arrival at the Finland Station, and wrote numerous articles analysing the current political situation and apportioning blame for the mistakes that were being made. Yet for all his energy and shrewdness, Sukhanov, in common with the other socialist leaders he criticized so bitterly, proved fatally incapable of affecting the events that really mattered.

Sukhanov had made a detailed study of Marxist theory, and he was certain of the path the revolution *ought* to follow. As early as Friday, 9 March he decided:

The Soviet democracy had to entrust the power to the propertied elements, its class enemy, without whose participation it could not now master the techniques of administration in the desperate conditions of disintegration.

He sympathized with the reluctance of the Petrograd proletariat to return to work under a bourgeois government, for:

The proletariat of the capital had only just begun living a new life; it was bound by hundreds of thousands of threads to all sorts of new organisations, and had only just managed to achieve for itself a new way of life from which it had to tear itself away for the old half-forgotten workbench.

He was adamant, however, that the demands of the masses for the Soviet immediately to seize power must be resisted at all costs, although he realized from the beginning the danger that the masses might not rest content with the establishment of the Provisional Government as the first stage on the long road to socialism. On 15 March, his friend's housekeeper, Anna Mikhailovna, told him:

The queues – well the queues haven't got smaller in the least; I think they're even bigger. You stand half the day, just as before. . . . They say, "liberty-flibberty, it's all the same, there's nothing to be had". They say it's just the same, "the rich keep on fleecing the poor. The shopkeepers are the only ones making money."

Sukhanov feared that the Bolsheviks might exploit this situation to seize power for themselves. Later in the month he buttonholed Kamenev, the first important Bolshevik leader to return from exile, and sought reassurance that:

You are not going to overthrow the bourgeois government yet and don't insist on an immediate democratic [socialist] regime.

He realized that with Lenin's arrival in April the Bolsheviks had become more dangerous, for:

There can be no doubt about it – Lenin is an extraordinary phenomenon, a man of absolutely exceptional intellectual power . . . he represents an unusually happy combination of theoretician and popular leader, who has the ability not only to seduce the masses, who have had no other teaching than that of the Tsarist whip, but also the Bolshevik Party itself.

With the benefit of hindsight, Sukhanov admitted that Lenin showed consummate skill in ignoring the "elementary foundations of Marxism and replacing them with demagogy, brazen and unbounded". He and his fellow democratic socialists, on the other hand, had stuck to a Marxist theory that proved "incomprehensible to the masses, who had just barely tasted the blessing of free political development". As a result, "the disappointed, weary and hungry masses swept over our heads".

Why could Sukhanov, with all his influential connections, do so little to head off the dangers he foresaw? Among the leading democratic socialists he proved to be more than usually impotent, hampered by a distaste for the cut and thrust of popular politics.

Although he spent endless hours in debate with intellectual colleagues:

I had no experience as an orator, wasn't used to addressing the masses and had no taste for it, which I often regretted very much.

Attaching much importance to hair-splitting ideological differences, he long avoided formal party membership with its inevitable compromises, and it is surely significant that he eventually joined a tiny splinter-group with no newspaper of its own and no representation in the Soviet.

There were, however, even deeper reasons for this impotence. Joel Carmichael, editor of Sukhanov's memoirs, has written:

Sukhanov's attitude towards the Bolsheviks illuminates the ambivalence that hamstrung so many of their opponents. As a socialist Sukhanov grew more and more indignant with the Bolsheviks as their intention of taking power became manifest.

At the same time, he could not deny that the Bolsheviks had secured a genuine mass following. It was, comments Carmichael:

Truly an insoluble problem. How indeed could Sukhanov reconcile his fidelity to the masses with his opinion that their actual goal under Bolshevik leadership was a fateful adventure implemented by unscrupulous means? How right he was to feel neglected by history!

Although, for example, Sukhanov felt that the Bolshevik demonstrations known as the July Days would harm the revolution, he also felt that:

independently of the political results, it was impossible to look on this stupendous movement of the masses with anything but enthusiasm. Even if you thought it was fatal, you could only rejoice in its gigantic elemental sweep.

When fellow socialists proposed outlawing the Bolshevik Party, Sukhanov vigorously opposed the suggestion, on the grounds that it would give fresh heart to the supporters of counter-revolution.

The futility of Sukhanov's 1917 career was brought home to him on the eve of the October Revolution. His apartment was eight versts (five miles) from the Tauride Palace, where the Soviet met. On the afternoon of 23

13 On the evening of 7 November 1917 Lenin announces the establishment of the world's first socialist government. This artist's impression was probably painted after Lenin's death, for it shows Stalin standing conspicuously behind Lenin, a position of prominence he did not warrant in 1917.

October his wife, Galina, who was a Bolshevik sympathizer, solicitously advised him not to bother coming home after the evening session of the Soviet but to sleep at the Tauride instead. Thus it was that while Sukhanov listened to speeches one of the world's most critical events took place at his own flat and without his knowledge, for it was here that the Bolshevik leadership met in secret and planned the insurrection of 7/8 November. Sukhanov himself did not see Lenin until the evening of 8 November, at Smolny, the Bolshevik Party headquarters, where he witnessed the Bolshevik leader's first triumphant public appearance after the coup and came face to face with his own personal and political tragedy. He recalled:

The entire praesidium [Bolshevik leadership], headed by Lenin, were standing up singing with excited exalted faces and blazing eyes . . . while the mass of delegates were permeated by the faith that all would go well in the future too. They were beginning to be persuaded of the communist peace, land and bread, and even beginning to feel some readiness to stand up for their newly acquired goods and rights . . .

But I didn't believe in the victory, the success, the "rightfulness" or the historical mission of a Bolshevik regime. Sitting in the back seats, I watched this celebration with a heavy heart. How I longed to join in and merge with this mass and its leaders in a single feeling. But I couldn't.

In spite of these misgivings, and without ever joining the Communist Party, Sukhanov co-operated with the new regime from 1918 onwards. When the British journalist, Arthur Ransome, met him in 1919, he was working in a Soviet economic-planning bureau. He told Ransome that, misguided though the Bolsheviks might be, socialists had no choice but to support them during the civil war, for:

there was a danger lest the agitation of the Mensheviks or others might set fire to the discontent of the masses against the actual physical conditions, and end in pogroms destroying Bolsheviks and Mensheviks alike.

In the relatively liberal atmosphere of the early 1920s, Sukhanov's memoirs were published in the Soviet Union. Perhaps predictably, however, he was one of the first victims of the campaign against political unorthodoxy waged by Stalin, the man whom Sukhanov had once publicly described as "a grey blur, looming up now and then dimly and not leaving any trace". In the so-called "Trial of the Mensheviks" in 1931, Sukhanov was accused of taking part in a conspiracy with the capitalist nations to "promote military intervention, destruction of the Soviet state and the restoration of capitalism". Condemned to a labour camp at Verkne-Uralsk in central Russia, he disappeared from history.

Vladimir Korostovetz

Vladimir Korostovetz was born into a wealthy, noble family with a long history of service to the Tsarist state. His father, a Guards officer of decidedly conservative views, continued in the family tradition, but his mother, Alexandra, had been educated abroad and dreamed of the day when autocratic Russia would be converted into a liberal, democratic state, on the Western European model. She employed an English tutor for her four sons, was active in the Zemstvo movement (a system of democratically elected local councils, responsible for local welfare) and disliked the duties she was expected to perform as the wife of an imperial officer, "with all the traditions and petty prejudices". During Vladimir's boyhood the family estate, Peresash, in the Chernigov district of the Ukraine, was a haven for all kinds of political dissidents. Several Social Democrats, hunted by the police, were employed as tutors, and:

Thus it was that Peresash came to be the meeting place for political suspects. In the evenings impromptu meetings and discussions would often be organised, and heated debates would follow every lecture on Herzen, Chernishevsky, Chekov, Tolstoy or Dostoyevsky. (V. Korstovetz, *Seed and Harvest*, London, 1931)

A neighbour once told Madame Korostovetz: "Your children will end in Siberia." In 1906 Uncle Ismael, Vice-Governor of Estonia, visited the family's St Petersburg house. For his part in liquidating the Baltic revolutionary movement Ismael had been condemned to death by a secret tribunal. Unknown to him, members of that very group were hiding from the police in the Korostovetz house. With loyalties divided, the family hid from each the knowledge of the other's presence, although the uncle did remark that:

queer people seemed to haunt his brother's house, queer people whose looks – long hair and general untidiness – suggested revolutionary ideas.

In preparation for the free Russia of the future, Alexandra believed that enlightened landowners should teach the peasants social responsibility and enthusiasm for democracy. Peasants on the Peresash estate, therefore, were given generous grants of land, had their welfare looked after and were encouraged to adopt modern farming techniques and co-operative marketing.

Connections in high places protected Madame Korostovetz from police prosecution, but other liberal landowners were not so fortunate. Among them was Vassily Khishniakov, a neighbour and Zemstvo worker, who "believed in a democratic Russia, believed in the Russian peasant and believed in the possibility of parliamentary achievements for a Tsarist Russia". In the reaction following the 1905 Revolution:

Such a creed alone was sufficient to place a highly educated and entirely harmless man on the black list of revolutionaries, to have him persecuted and dragged before the courts, exiled and, in a word, to give him the reputation of being "red" and have him kept under continual supervision.

Vladimir Korostovetz was deeply influenced by his mother's views. After a meeting with Lenin in 1908, however, he rejected the revolutionary path to change as unrealistic, for:

At the time I considered it most improbable that such a madman would ever find an opportunity of coming to grips with real facts or could ever obtain power.

He joined the liberal Cadet Party, and all his hopes came to be centred on:

the State Duma [a parliament established after the 1905 Revolution] and the statesmanlike personalities in it who were to build up the Russia of the future, and I was unable to imagine that the anarchistic students and the little party of emigrants in a foreign country could ever succeed in overthrowing Russia.

The outbreak of war in 1914 found Korostovetz employed as a Foreign Office civil servant. He hoped, at first, that the war would lead to a "strengthening of the parliamentary system", although, like most liberals, he looked forward to the reform rather than the abolition of the monarchy. The Tsar's stubborn refusal to co-operate with the Duma and the corruption and incompetence of the War Cabinets, however, destroyed these hopes, and by 1916:

The Duma circles and public organizations were

14 The Duma in session in 1906. Disillusioned deputies formed the hub of the first Provisional Government.

irritated by the failure of all their hopes, and the closing of the Duma and the dismissal of the liberal ministers was looked upon as a challenge, so that they openly prepared to take steps against the Government and their plans were made without sparing the Imperial family, including the Tsar.

In the event, Vladimir Korostovetz had profound misgivings about the way in which the February Revolution finally came about. The spontaneous upsurge in the streets of Petrograd was very different from the orderly transfer of power envisaged by the liberals. Yet he could not help seeing the revolution as "the fulfilment of my mother's ideals" and, in spite of himself, was infected by the heady atmosphere of those early days.

As secretary to Foreign Minister, Miliukov between March and May 1917, Korostovetz had an intimate view of the weakness of the Provisional Government and the increasing radicalization and violence of the revolution. He and his wife hid several officers threatened by the men under their command, and on one occasion his own life was in danger from arbitrary violence:

as I happened to be using my telephone near the window, I saw a drunken sailor in the street, decorated with machine-gun belts – at that moment the acme of revolutionary smartness – taking aim at me. I was only just able to jump away from the window, and the bullet struck the woodwork.

His faith in the ultimate triumph of democracy did not waver, however, and when the Bolsheviks seized power, he remained convinced that "the rule of such people cannot be of long duration in Russia". The civil service strike of November/December 1917, in which Korostovetz took part, was prompted by the fallacious belief that the Bolsheviks could be deposed by "the united power of the official intelligentsia" and the Constituent Assembly convened. When the veteran Socialist Revolutionary, Chaikovsky

remarked sadly how he had spent the greater part of his life as a political exile, and that it looked as though he were to finish his days in like manner – but this time in consequence of the extremism of the Left and the tyranny of the Lenin crowd,

23

Korostovetz thought he was being unduly pessimistic, for:

the rest of us had not yet awakened out of our dreams in which we saw a free Russia on the road of progress.

When the strike disintegrated, Korostovetz returned to Peresash, hoping that the dream of democracy might still be preserved in rural Russia:

I placed all my hopes in the independence of local political organisations – Zemstvo, Union of Zemstvo and Towns, the Co-operative movement. . . . I was closely connected with the Co-operative movement, for my mother had assisted the peasants attached to it with gifts of wood, bricks, land and money, in the hope that even the most primitive economic independence would evoke in them a desire for the development of culture and democracy.

He had nothing but contempt for landowners who fled from rural violence and joined reactionary movements designed to bring about a total return to the old days. Such people, reasoned Korostovetz, had failed to come to grips with "the underlying reasons for the revolution, not grasping the fact that life, like a river, cannot flow backwards". Among the peasants of Peresash he aimed to foster a spirit of co-operativeness and social responsibility, so that together they might defend the estate against the prevailing anarchy and create a miniature model democracy. Education was a vital part of this process:

I tried to get the peasants to take an interest in the development of social work as opposed to pogroms and extremism. I kept in close touch with the estate employees, organised lectures for them and generally followed all their ideas. At the same time I took an interest in co-operative matters, for it appeared . . . that only in this way could the primitive peasants be brought to work for themselves and the common weal.

After a while, the ownership of the estate was handed over to a committee chosen by the peasants themselves, and the Korostovetz family henceforth counted themselves as employees. In time, they hoped, the example of Peresash would spread throughout the district and a third force be created, that would be strong enough to hold out against Red and White tyranny alike.

At first, all went well. In early 1918 the Chernigov Bolsheviks were local people, who:

knew us as a liberal family about whom my mother had created a kind of halo for her unending work for the peasants; so that they did not really believe in the denunciations made by disgruntled peasants against the "landowner burjuis" [bourgeois]. Thus we had secret friends in these circles rather than open enemies.

However, when the Bolsheviks re-occupied the Ukraine in December 1918, after eight months of German occupation, commissars from Moscow and Petrograd came with them, who were unacquainted with local conditions and rigidly doctrinaire. Even the hospital for wounded soldiers, established at Peresash in 1914, became a liability, for:

We were accused of making millions by means of it and of thus appropriating the property of the

15 Class hatred in the rural areas hit liberal and oppressive landlords alike. Here Bolshevik supporters begin the destruction of a country estate.

people; yet all expenses of the hospital were met solely by my mother, who did not receive one penny from the state.

While most, though not all, of the Peresash peasantry remained loyal, other local peasants joined in the Bolshevik vendetta against the landowners, and another, equally liberal neighbour was murdered by his own tenants. When Bolshevik troops, accompanied by revengeful peasants, surrounded Peresash, the Korostovetz family decided to flee to Polish territory, and during six months of flight and concealment Vladimir's mother and two of his brothers were killed. Alexandra Korostovetz had indeed courted death by refusing to adopt an alias, for:

She was always convinced that as she had spent her life in founding schools for the peasants and hospitals for wounded soldiers in all the villages of our estate the people would not harm us.

When Denikin captured nearby Poltava in the summer of 1919, she and her eldest son were taken prisoner by the Cheka (the Communist secret police, established in December 1918) and were shot, tragic victims of the failure of liberalism and the triumph of extremism in backward Russia. Vladimir Korostovetz and his wife eventually reached the Polish-held city of Minsk and began a life-long exile in Warsaw and Berlin.

Alexander Lukomsky (1868-1939)

At the outbreak of revolution Alexander Lukomsky was a senior general, holding the post of Director of Military Operations at the Stavka (Headquarters) of the Supreme Commander-in-Chief in Moghilev. His initial reaction to the political developments was that of an old-fashioned patriot and of a soldier preoccupied with military concerns. At all costs, the war with Germany must be pursued to a victorious conclusion, and if that meant abandoning the Romanov dynasty and accepting the Provisional Government, then Lukomsky found that a relatively easy decision to make. When the generals at the Stavka realized how serious the disturbances in Petrograd really were, he counselled against sending an army to the capital, for:

It was . . . evident that a decision to crush the revolution by force of arms would also cause

16 General Alexander Lukomsky.

17 Fraternization between German and Russian soldiers in 1917. By the end of the year morale and discipline in the Russian army had completely evaporated.

great bloodshed in Petrograd and Moscow, and also threatened to put an end to our struggle against the enemy at the Front; this decision would also only be possible if we concluded a shameful and dishonourable peace with Germany first. This, however, was such an awful prospect that it seemed as though anything· ought to be done to end the revolution peacefully, so long as the war could be carried on. (*Memoirs of the Russian Revolution,* London, 1922)

What Lukomsky eventually found intolerable was the disintegration of morale and discipline in the army between March and August 1917. Indeed, so depressed did he become at the inability of the General Staff to stop this process that in April he requested a transfer to an active command. His experiences with the 1st Army Corps on the Northern Front only deepened his fears, however:

From the very first days of my command I realised that I would not be commander of a corps but "Persuader-in-Chief". . . . I daily received the most pessimistic reports from the commanders of divisions, who complained that the newly-formed committees interfered with everything, that the men refused to go through

the usual practice and drill, while the commanding staff were deprived of inflicting any disciplinary punishment on them for the insubordination . . .

The vicinity of Petrograd made itself felt. All the propaganda and agitation issued in the capital under the form of proclamations, appeals, leaflets, brochures etc. was received and circulated among the regiments of our corps on the next day after their appearing. Propagandists appeared almost daily on our premises. At the end of April, when Lenin began his fatal activity in the capital, this propaganda grew still more intensive.

His conviction that the weak Provisional Government was only playing into the hands of the Bolsheviks made of Lukomsky an active participant in the Kornilov conspiracy. His account of those confused September days is only one of a number of conflicting versions by men eager to justify their actions, and it cannot, therefore, be accepted uncritically. Yet there is little reason to doubt that Lukomsky sincerely believed Kornilov to be without personal ambitions and desirous only of "saving Russia and the world".

Involvement in the Kornilov Affair earned Lukomsky and other generals a fairly comfortable imprisonment in a former Catholic monastery at Bykhov. When the Bolsheviks seized power, however, the generals feared for their lives, and on 12 December they escaped in a variety of disguises:

Romanovsky was turned into a sub-lieutenant of the engineering troops; Maslov dressed as a soldier; Denikin and I changed our military clothes for civilian ones. I shaved off my beard and moustache. Suitable documents and passports had been prepared beforehand.

Always in danger of recognition, Lukomsky made his way south. On one occasion:

I ran across my former orderly, who had been sent away from Bykhov at my request for his open Bolshevik tendencies. The soldier stopped, glanced at my polushubok [sheepskin coat], which was well-known to him, and then at my face. I was clean-shaven, with dark eyeglasses, and made a grimace in order not to be recognised. I cannot tell whether he recognised me or not, but he gave a strange whistle and jumped on to the train which was approaching the station.

In Don Cossack territory, Lukomsky joined the former Commander-in-Chief, Alekseev, in trying to create a Volunteer Army to expel the Bolsheviks. Recruiting was difficult – plenty of officers volunteered but few soldiers – and so was supply. Hoped-for Allied aid was slow to materialize. At the turn of the year 1917-18 representatives of the British and French military missions promised a grant of ten million roubles a month, starting in January 1918, but nothing was actually received for many months. Volunteers for the White Army were often little more than adventurers – "sometimes simply brigands – who had only their own profit and gain in view, and plundered the population."

During the short-lived Bolshevik occupation of the Don region early in 1919, Lukomsky and his friend General Ronjin, were captured by a Bolshevik detachment. Their journey to the railway station, where they were to be tried before a revolutionary tribunal, was terrifying. Lukomsky recalled:

We reached the station before dawn, but the news of our arrival immediately spread as if by magic, and the waiting room of the first class, into which we were led, rapidly filled with tovarishtchi [comrades]. It was clear that a miracle alone could save us. We were surrounded by men little better than wild beasts, who clamoured for blood and did not wish to wait for the decision of the tribunal. . . . The commander of the military detachment at the station, Stepnaia, who was at the same time president of the military tribunal, had the greatest difficulty in persuading them to let the trial take place.

Yet it was clear that the Red Army was no longer just a rabble but on the way to becoming a disciplined force with commanders of stature. The detachment commander insisted, against all the odds, on a proper trial, and when the accused were unexpectedly acquitted, protected them from a lynching.

The spring of 1919 saw Lukomsky reunited with the Volunteer Army, now under a new commander, General Denikin, and enjoying an upsurge in its fortunes. While the Bolsheviks were being driven from the Don and the Ukraine, Lukomsky was appointed President of the "Special Council" attached to Denikin's armies. This was responsible for formulating the political programme of the southern Whites. Writing in 1922, Lukomsky appeared as bewildered then as he must have been in 1919 as to what would have been the best slogans to adopt, for:

I do not believe that any conscientious political leader, whatever party he may belong to, can be able, as yet, to say what line of conduct it was necessary to follow, what political device it was necessary to proclaim, in order to win the sympathy of the popular masses in Russia. . .

The proclamation of a monarchist device in 1918 or 1919 would not have met with the sympathy, either of the Intelligentsia or of the peasant or labour masses. The fascination of revolution was still in the air, and a device of this kind would have signified "counter-revolution" and a return to the old regime. . .

As to the proclamation of republican ideas, this would have rendered it impossible to form a more or less serious or reliable army; the officers of the former regime, who had experienced all the bitterness of the revolution, would not have followed us on that line.

Effective civilian government in the areas occupied by the Whites, was made doubly difficult by a shortage of money and personnel; Lukomsky complained:

Partly owing to the small choice of suitable candidates and partly to the low rate of salary, these nominations were very difficult, and it often happened that responsible posts were filled with people who either could not master the work or

18 Cossack soldiers, often reluctant allies of the White armies.

else took bribes from the population and shut their eyes to all kinds of abuses.

The problems were real enough, but, in addition, Lukomsky proved an honest but inept politician. He accepted wholeheartedly Denikin's "Great Russia" concept and found it impossible to compromise with Cossack demands for autonomy, for:

It was evident that once there existed an independent sovereign state of the Cossacks of the Don, the political leaders of the Kuban would tend, in their turn, to separate themselves entirely from the command of the Volunteer Army. It was to be feared that some of these leaders would insist on the creation of an independent state of the Kuban. . . . Their chief aim and object was to form a union of several independent states in the south-east of Russia.

To Russian patriots like Denikin and Lukomsky such a price was too high to pay, even for enthusiastic Cossack participation in the crusade against the Bolsheviks.

Writing in 1922, Lukomsky was dealing with events that were still close and people who were still alive. Understandably, his account of the disorderly retreat of the White army is low-key and confined mainly to the bare facts. It is not difficult, however, for a perceptive reader to catch glimpses of the personal animosities that defeat engendered among Denikin's staff. One of the Commander-in-Chief's final actions was to appoint General Shilling, who had gravely mismanaged the evacuation of Odessa, to command the troops in the Crimea, last stronghold of the Whites. This appointment, Lukomsky recalled, provoked "strong indignation among both the older and younger officers" and a conspiracy was formed to replace Shilling with General Wrangel. For taking part in this plot, Lukomsky was sacked by Denikin, and his disillusionment shines through his bald statement that "I was now free and had the right to be evacuated with my family".

When Lukomsky wrote his memoirs in exile in Constantinople, the Volunteer Army had been completely expelled from Russian territory, but he did not accept the defeat as final. The retreat from the Crimea, he was sure, was a tactical manoeuvre allowing Wrangel to save the army "for the further regeneration of Russia, and as an invaluable national cadre for the future Russian army".

LIFE IN REVOLUTIONARY RUSSIA

Revolution and civil war completed the destruction of economic life and social relationships that the 1914 war had begun. The food shortages in the cities, that had sparked off the February Revolution, were greatly exacerbated by the collapse of centralized authority. It is no coincidence that the Bolsheviks won a majority in the Soviet only days after the city's bread ration was halved, and Lenin's followers rode into power on a wave of enthusiasm that a dramatic improvement in urban living conditions would automatically follow the seizure of power by the proletariat.

Reality soon intervened. The popular slogan that food shortages were due to evil speculators could not produce regular supplies, when the real problems were rural chaos and a rapidly-decaying transport network. There was no possibility that the Bolsheviks could even begin to remedy so complex a situation in the face of civil war, and the problems were made much worse by the White control of the major grain-growing areas between 1918 and 1920. For three long years economic reconstruction was postponed, while all remaining resources were bled white in the cause of supplying the Red Army. This was "war Communism", the mobilization of the entire active population behind the war effort. Among its features were forced labour and conscription, the requisitioning of surplus grain from the peasants and a strict rationing system; an order even went out in 1920 that all women between the ages of eighteen and forty-five were to sew underwear for the Red Army. To ensure the success of war Communism, a mixture of coercion and bribery was used. The lion's share of the scarce resources was concentrated on those groups on whose support Bolshevism most depended. The food-card system, for example, divided the population into categories according to function and class. Red Army men, including co-opted former Tsarist officers, and manual workers fell into the top two categories; white-collar employees of the Soviet regime fell into category three; those members of the old ruling class who could not find employment received no official rations at all. As even the best rations fell considerably short of what was

19 Bartering personal possessions for food. Those excluded by the strict rationing system of war Communism had no alternative but to rely on the Black Market. (From *Engravings of the Great War* by H.W. Wilson, published in 1919.)

needed to avoid malnutrition, the grim reality faced by many who remained in Bolshevik territory during the civil war is plain to see. That any from the least privileged classes survived at all was owing to the operation of a black market, to which the authorities often turned a blind eye (the Sukharevka Market in Moscow, for example, functioned until 1920), and to a mass exodus to the countryside. By 1921 the population of Petrograd had fallen to one third of its pre-war level.

Moreover, class hatred was deliberately used by the Bolsheviks as an economic and political weapon. Committees of the Poor, organized by commissars sent out from the cities, urged poor peasants to seize grain from their richer neighbours and donate it to the Red Army. Urban workers were given apartments in expropriated houses; in Odessa Elisaveta Fen witnessed the evacuation of an entire middle-class district and its resettlement by families from working-class suburbs. There was free travel on public transport for soldiers and workers. An efficient propaganda machine kept alive memories of the Cossack whips of 1905. The Red Terror run by the Cheka was a class terror. Its victims included not only those caught in acts of counter-revolution and Communists found guilty of corruption or desertion, but also many hostages whose only crime was their class. A new kind of tension crept into social relationships and no chance acquaintance could ever fully be trusted.

There was a positive side to Communism too. A valiant attempt was made to establish the equality and dignity of the working man. Some unjust social conventions, including the inferior status of women and the illegitimate, were abolished in law. Gross inequalities of wealth were outlawed. People's Commissars (ministers) were paid five hundred roubles a month, which put them on the wage level of a skilled worker. Particular stress was laid on the right of working people to education. The state publishing house undertook to print all the great Russian classics in cheap editions, and university lectures were thrown open to all, although a Soviet official told Arthur Ransome that in the era of shortages "there are more projects than realisation of projects".

In the White-controlled areas food supplies were more plentiful, but corruption was rampant, and the hope of a brighter future that characterized the Communist camp even in its darkest hours was missing. There was less organized terror, but the ill-disciplined troops of Denikin and Kolchak were guilty of spontaneous outbursts of violence, not only against suspected "Reds", but also against traditionally unpopular minorities such as Jews. While one's chances of survival in the Red areas depended often on class, among the Whites, especially during the disorderly retreats from Omsk and Rostov, it was the fittest who survived.

Subsistence-level existence and large movements of population bred terrifying epidemics of cholera and typhus; nine million died between 1918 and 1921 of cold, famine and disease. By the time Bolshevik rule was firmly established, Russia was in ruins. An attempt to rebuild the economy by an intensification of war Communism and the conversion of the Red Army into labour battalions failed to inspire even the working class, whose energies had at last been drained by prolonged privation. Loyal Communists such as the Kronstadt sailors resented that Party dictatorship, once justified as a temporary necessity, had not been eased. Requisitioning detachments sent to wrest the last grain of wheat from the peasants could not disguise the fact that disgruntled farmers were simply not growing enough to feed the cities. The Kronstadt and Tambov uprisings of 1921 were clear indications that war Communism had out-lived its usefulness and a change of course was imperative.

Louise Bryant

Although American journalist, Louise Bryant, classed herself as a "socialist", she arrived in Russia in September 1917, six months after she had first read about the February Revolution in a New York evening paper, with little knowledge of the factions into which Russian socialism had split or of the particular social and economic conditions in which the revolutionaries operated. Her credentials as a foreign "comrade" gave her easy access to most of the leading politicians of the Left and allowed her to move freely among the ordinary people of Petrograd, and she rapidly became swept along on the wave of popular enthusiasm that was to bring the Bolsheviks to power. Her emotional account of her first six months in Russia provides a valuable personal insight into the tumultuous forces that destroyed the Provisional Government.

Petrograd in the autumn of 1917 was a city threatened by famine. Louise noticed:

the long lines of scantily-clad people standing in the bitter cold waiting to buy bread, sugar or tobacco. From four o'clock in the morning they begin to stand there, while it is still black night. Often after standing in line for hours the supplies run out. Most of the time only one-fourth pound of bread for two days is allowed. (*Six Red Months in Russia*, London, 1982)

War-weariness was evident everywhere. At

20 Petrograd during the October Revolution.

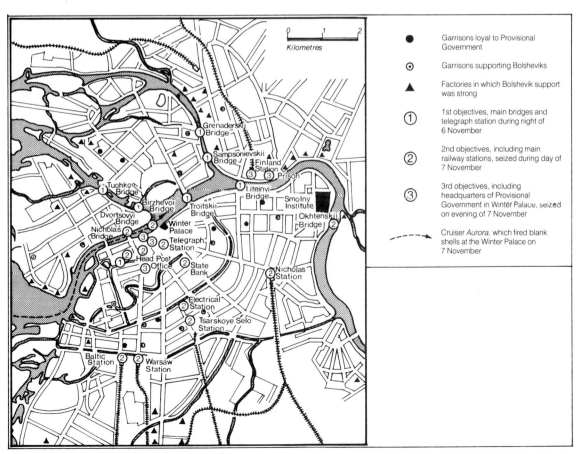

●	Garrisons loyal to Provisional Government
⊙	Garrisons supporting Bolsheviks
▲	Factories in which Bolshevik support was strong
①	1st objectives, main bridges and telegraph station during night of 6 November
②	2nd objectives, including main railway stations, seized during day of 7 November
③	3rd objectives, including headquarters of Provisional Government in Winter Palace, seized on evening of 7 November
- - - ➤	Cruiser *Aurora*, which fired blank shells at the Winter Palace on 7 November

Map labels: Grenaderskii Bridge, Sampsonievskii Bridge, Finland Station, Prison, Tuohkov Bridge, Liteinyi Bridge, Smolny Institute, Birzhevoi Bridge, Troitskii Bridge, Okhtenskii Bridge, Dvortsovyi Bridge, Winter Palace, Nicholas Bridge, Telegraph Station, Head Post Office, State Bank, Nicholas Station, Electrical Station, Tsarskoye Selo Station, Baltic Station, Warsaw Station

Kilometres 0 1 2

21 A bread queue in Petrograd, 1917.

Smolny, headquarters of the Bolshevik Party, Louise first witnessed a scene that was to become familiar to her over the next few months:

A tired, emaciated little soldier mounts the rostrum. He is covered with mud from head to foot and with old bloodstains. He blinks in the glaring light. It is the first speech he has ever made and he begins it in a shrill hysterical shout:
"Tavarishi! (comrades) I come from the place where men are digging their graves and calling them trenches! We are forgotten out there in the snow and cold. We are forgotten while you sit here and discuss politics! I tell you the army can't fight much longer . . . I tell you something's got to be done or the soldiers are going home."

Few workers or soldiers believed any longer in the Provisional Government, although Kerensky himself could still sway an audience with his personal charisma and powerful oratory. In October Louise Bryant witnessed him in action:

Only persons of great intensity can make an audience hold its breath in just the way Kerensky did as he walked quickly across the stage. He was clad in a plain brown soldier's suit without so much as a brass button or an epaulette to mark him Commander-in-Chief of the Russian army and navy and Minister-President of the Russian Republic. Somehow all this unpretentiousness accentuated the dignity of his position. . . . Deeply conscious of the coldness, the hostility even of his audience, he played on it skilfully with oratory, with pleading, with a strange unabated inward energy. His face and his voice became tragic and desolate, changed slowly and became firelit, radiating, triumphant; before the magnificent range of his emotion all opposition was at last swept away.

His speeches, however, were full of empty words and evaded the crucial issues; "an hour after his departure his influence was gone." Eventually, Kerensky himself realized that it was all a sham. During one of the last speeches he made before the October Revolution, "he was so overcome with the hopelessness of the situation that he rushed from the platform, and having gained his seat, wept openly before the whole assembly."

It was to the Bolshevik Party that the disillusioned turned for relief, a development that Louise Bryant greeted with enthusiasm. She did not, as did many of her contemporaries, see Lenin and Trotsky as skilful opportunists but as men:

borne along on the whirlwind of radicalism that

22 Kerensky (left) saluting troops as they leave for the front, summer 1917. Such gestures did little to halt the disintegration of the Russian army.

swept and is still sweeping Russia and they themselves did not know how long or how well they would be able to ride that whirlwind.

She spent most of her time at Smolny and watched:

it change from a lonely deserted place into a busy humming hive, heart and soul of the last revolution. . . . In the cavernous dark hallways where here and there flickered a pale electric light, thousands and thousands of soldiers and sailors and factory workers tramped in their heavy, mud-covered boots every day. . . . Smolny worked twenty four hours a day. For weeks Trotsky never left the building. He ate and slept and worked in his office on the third floor and strings of people came in every hour of the day to see him. All the leaders were frightfully over-worked, they looked haggard and pale from loss of sleep.

As October passed, huge caches of rifles were stacked along the walls and it was obvious to any observer that insurrection was being planned.

With the Provisional Government so discredited, the actual seizure of Petrograd by the Bolsheviks was relatively bloodless and good-natured. Louise wrangled her way into the Winter Palace in the hours before it was captured by the Red Guard. There she found a government paralysed by a sense of helplessness. When the Palace surrendered, the cadets who were supposed to be defending it looked only "relieved that it was all over". What little resistance there was was quickly diffused by the energy and decisiveness of the Bolsheviks. Kerensky, who had escaped from the capital, tried to raise an army among the Cossack regiments at the Front. It was rumoured that the armoured-car division, stationed in Petrograd, would join them if they came. Louise Bryant witnessed the debate that took place at the barracks. Just as it seemed as if the vote would go in Kerensky's favour:

a stocky little man climbed up the sides of the car. He had short legs and a large head and

23 Red Guards storm the Winter Palace, 7 November 1917. The takeover turned out to be almost bloodless.

sharp, squinting little eyes. It was Krylenko [a prominent Bolshevik and future war commissar]. For two nights he had not slept, and he had but a few minutes before arrived on a train from the front. His face was so white and he looked so tired that it seemed foolish to bother about him. His cause seemed hopeless. Then he began to speak. . . . As his voice rose over that huddled crowd of soldiers the atmosphere changed rapidly. Men began to move around, to argue with one another; there was no more polite silence, eyes flashed. He talked for about fifteen minutes. When he finished there was no applause but a great roar, "All power to the soviets!" Krylenko stepped back smiling and showed his teeth in a tired grin. The chairman came forward and asked for the vote. There were three thousand soldiers; all but twenty five went with Krylenko.

Although the October Revolution was made by the urban poor, the early days, when the spirit of idealism was still strong, produced relatively little hooliganism or arbitrary violence. When the Winter Palace surrendered:

Everyone leaving the Palace was searched no matter on what side he was. There were priceless treasures all about and it was a great temptation to pick up souvenirs. I have always been glad I was present that night because so many stories have come out about the looting. . . .

A young Bolshevik lieutenant stood by the only unlocked door, and in front of him was a great table. Two soldiers did the searching. The lieutenant delivered a kind of sermon while this was going on. I wrote down part of his speech: "Comrades, this is the people's palace. Do not steal from the people. . . . Do not disgrace the people."

In January 1918 mobs of soldiers looted the city's wine cellars and ran amok. Serious violence was prevented, however, by the disciplined Kronstadt sailors, who executed the ringleaders and poured the alcohol stocks into the canals, so that "the snow was rose-stained and the city reeked with stale alcohol".

Louise Bryant left Russia in the early months of 1918, completely won over to Bolshevism. From the calm of neutral Sweden she gazed eastwards in the direction from which she had come:

I was homesick for my own country, but I thought of the German advance and my heart ached. I wanted to go back and offer my life for the revolution.

Arthur Ransome (1884-1967)

Although Arthur Ransome is best-known in England as a writer of children's fiction, one of his earliest enthusiasms was for Russian folktales. On his first visit to that country in 1913, he learned the rudiments of the language and collected the material for *Old Peter's Russian Tales*, published in 1916. The outbreak of war in 1914 found him once again in Petrograd, this time as a freelance correspondent for the *Daily News* and *Manchester Guardian*; he remained there until the summer of 1918 and made the acquaintance of many leading revolutionaries. In January 1919 he paid a brief visit to the Bolshevik-controlled areas and recorded his impressions in *Six Weeks in Russia*, published in June of the same year.

Ransome believed that he had got "as near as any foreigner who was not a Communist could get to what was going on"; he was "far removed in origin and upbringing from revolutionary and socialist movements" and was convinced that he could therefore judge events more objectively than most. In the introduction to his book he wrote:

I have tried by means of a bald record of conversations held and things seen to provide material for those who wish to know what is being done and thought in Moscow at the present time, and demand something more to go upon than second-hand reports of wholly irrelevant atrocities committed by either one side or the other.

These claims cannot be accepted without qualification. Ransome's experience of Russia in 1919 was confined to Moscow and Petrograd, where Bolshevik control was undisputed; he saw nothing of the frontier areas, where civil war still raged and passions ran high. He was easily duped by Bolshevik propaganda and self-delusion. When he told Sereda, Commissar for Agriculture, that he had heard that peasants were refusing to sow more crops than they needed for their own use, he was told, and readily accepted, that "on the contrary, the latest reports gave them the right to hope for a greater sown area this year than ever before", a claim that was very far from the truth. Yet, for all its limitations,

Six Weeks in Russia stands as a vivid and honest account of one man's view of Soviet Russia fourteen months on from the October Revolution.

Outside Russia wild rumours circulated of privation, atrocities and political upheavals in the Bolshevik-controlled cities. The Finnish lieutenant who accompanied Ransome and his fellow journalists to the frontier post chattered:

good-humouredly in Swedish and German, much as a man might think it worthwhile to be kind to a crowd of unfortunates just about to be flung into a boiling cauldron.

To Ransome, however, the Petrograd of 1919 appeared strangely calm after the turbulent years of 1917 and 1918, and Bolshevik rule there no longer seemed to depend on armed forces. This impression was strengthened three days later when the party reached Moscow, now the capital of Russia, where Ransome was to spend the bulk of his visit. A year ago, he recalled:

we lived with exhilaration or despair on a volcano which might any day erupt and sweep away the new life before anyone had become accustomed to live it.

Now:

The danger to the revolution was hundreds of miles away on the various fronts. Here, in the centre, the revolution was an established fact. People had ceased to wonder when it would end, were settling into their places in the new social order, and took their pleasures not as if they were plucking flowers on their way to execution, but in the ordinary routine of life.

The new reality was very different from the old. Overt class distinctions had all but disappeared. At the opera, for example:

The Moscow plutocracy of bald merchants and bejewelled fat wives had gone. Gone with them were evening dresses and white shirt fronts. The whole audience was in the monotone of everyday clothes.

Ransome was struck by the enthusiasm with which the masses absorbed the culture long denied them by the old regime:

Looking from face to face that night I thought there were very few people in the theatre who had had anything like a good dinner to digest. But, as for their keenness, I can imagine few audiences to which, from an actor's point of view, it would be better worthwhile to play.

Political life, too, had changed; leaders now shared the hardships of the led. Ransome once had dinner at Smolny and found it a very simple affair:

The Commissars, men and women, came in from their work, took their places, fed and went back to work again, Zinoviev in particular only staying a few minutes. The meal was extremely simple, soup with shreds of horseflesh in it, very good indeed, followed by a little kashka [buckwheat porridge] together with small slabs of some sort of white stuff of no particular consistency or taste. Then tea and a lump of sugar.

The acute fuel shortage also affected civilians and high government officials alike. Pavlovitch, President of the Committee for State Constructions, had lost the use of his right hand, whose fingers were "swollen and immovable" like "the roots of a vegetable", as a result of prolonged sedentary work in unheated rooms.

If life in Bolshevik Russia was more just than life in the past, it was also gruellingly hard. A rationing system designed to outlaw speculation and distribute necessities fairly could not conceal the stark fact that all commodities were in desperately short supply. Ransome's ration card entitled him to one meal a day of soup together with a morsel of meat or fish. He developed his own method of dealing with hunger:

One could obtain this meal at any time between

two and seven. Living hungrily through the morning, at two o'clock I used to experience definite relief in the knowledge that at any moment I could have my meal. Feeling in this way less hungry, I used then to postpone it hour by hour, and actually dined about five or six o'clock.

Gruesome sights were seen on the streets:

On the third day after my arrival in Moscow I saw a man driving a sledge laden with, I think, horseflesh, mostly bones, probably dead sledge horses. As he drove, a black crowd of crows followed the sledge and perched on it, tearing greedily at the meat. He beat at them continually with his whip, but they were so famished that they took no notice whatever.

The constructive work undertaken by the commissariats (ministries) was continually frustrated by shortages and the demands of the civil war. Free education for all, up to university level, had been introduced, but reality fell far short of these ambitious plans. The porter at Ransome's hotel described how his two sons went daily to school, "sing the Marseillaise, have dinner and come home". When Ransome confronted Pokrovsky, an official in the Education Commissariat, with this story, he was told:

It is perfectly true. We have not enough transport to feed the armies, let alone bring food and warmth to ourselves. And if, under these conditions, we forced children to go through all their lessons we should have corpses to teach, not children. But by making them come for their meals we do two things, keep them alive, and keep them in the habit of coming, so that when the warm weather comes we can do better.

Pavlovitch, in charge of a scheme for modernizing Russia's transport and power-supply systems, complained:

You know our plans. But with fighting on all our fronts, and with all our best men away, we are compelled to use 90% of our energy and materials for the immediate needs of the army . . . for example, Trotsky telegraphs here simply: "We shall be in Orenburg in two days", leaving us to do what is necessary. Then, with the map before me, I have to send what will be needed, no matter what useful work has to be abandoned elsewhere, engineers, railway gangs for putting right the railways, material for bridges and so on.

25 Lenin addressing soldiers in Moscow in 1920. His faith in the future of Soviet Communism rarely wavered.

24 Grain requisitioned under war Communism arriving at a railhead. In fact, only enough food reached the cities between 1918 and 1921 to maintain the barest subsistence level.

Yet the Bolshevik leadership remained hopeful about the future. Lenin, with whom Ransome secured an intimate interview, was utterly convinced that England was on the "eve of revolution" and he almost overwhelmed the more sceptical Englishman with his optimism. On his walk home from the Kremlin, Ransome pondered on what made Lenin tick:

More than ever Lenin struck me as a happy man. . . . I tried to think of any other man of his calibre who had a similar joyous temperament. I could think of no one. . . . I think the reason must be that he is the first great leader who utterly discounts the value of his own personality. . . . More than that, he believes, as a Marxist, in the movement of the masses which, with or without him, would still move. . . . He does not believe that any man could make or stop the revolution, which he thinks inevitable. . . . He is consequently free with a freedom no other great man has ever had.

Six weeks in Soviet Russia left Ransome so exhausted that "I began to fear rather than to seek new experiences and impressions." Yet he was also immensely impressed by "the creative effort of the revolution . . . that extraordinary vitality which obstinately persists in Moscow even in these dark days of discomfort, disillusion, pestilence, starvation and unwanted war". And his judgement was not altogether unsound. Although the civil war drew nearer to Moscow and Petrograd in the course of 1919 and famine intensified, Russia's two largest cities remained doggedly loyal to Communism and provided the secure base from which Bolshevik power could spread countrywide.

Olga Chernov

In the year from March 1917 to March 1918 Olga Chernov, wife of a leading Socialist Revolutionary politician, experienced dramatic changes of fortune. Returning from exile in Italy in July 1917, she was fêted as the wife of a popular Minister of Agriculture. On one occasion, accompanied by her youngest daughter, Ariane, she was listening to her husband address the crowd, when:

Someone called out: "Chernov's daughter is there!" They held out their arms and lifted her up, passing her from hand to hand over their heads. She was wearing a red dress which ballooned in the wind, and with her fair curls flying loose, she looked just like a flag. . . . At the end of his speech Victor was carried to our car through madly cheering crowds, with the band playing a triumphant revolutionary hymn. (*New Horizons,*

Reminiscences of the Russian Revolution, Plymouth, 1936)

This adulation, however, was short-lived. As a member of the Provisional Government, Victor Chernov was inescapably connected with the procrastination over land redistribution that lost the government the support of the peasants. In the autumn of 1917 Olga toured the rural areas around Petrograd and visited a village in which, the day before, the local landowner's house had been ransacked and burnt and his overseer thrown into the fire. Here she came face to face with the class war that was to destroy the ideals of moderate, democratic, middle-class socialists.

"But why destroy things which would have been useful? Why did you burn that poor man alive?" I

26 and 27 Olga and Victor Chernov.

asked curiously. . . . A soldier looked fixedly at me. "We shall build other gardens and other houses, but this time they'll be for ourselves", he said slowly.

"But it'll take years, hundreds of years to rebuild all this!" I cried, trying hard to make them see my point.

"Ah, that's what your class will never understand. We've got to make a clean sweep of the past and begin all over again. But you leave us to do things our own way, Missus. We know what we want and we mean to get it this time.

Victor Chernov opposed the Bolshevik Revolution as a flagrant breach of democratic principles and, in common with other Socialist Revolutionaries, retained a naive faith in the determination of the peasant masses to oppose the new dictatorship. When a Socialist Revolutionary majority was elected to the Constituent Assembly in January 1918, it seemed inevitable that the Bolsheviks should bow to the will of the majority and create a broadly-based coalition government. Few reckoned with Lenin's determination to use whatever force was necessary to maintain the Bolshevik victory. Chernov was elected President of the Assembly for its first session

28 1917. A country house is plundered by peasants and army deserters. (From *The Graphic*, 1917.)

that opened in January 1918, but could barely speak in the face of heckling from the Red Guard who had crowded into the hall. Olga recalled:

The hall began to resemble a battlefield. Chairs and tables were overturned, pictures torn from the walls, in every row there were groups of soldiers trying to heckle the speakers, their rifles cocked menacingly towards the platform. The sailors' faces were distorted with rage, they seemed almost inhuman. Their attitude was menacing, their impatient, feverish hands never left the trigger.

When the session finally broke up after only a day a leading Bolshevik warned Victor: "You'd better go out by the secret door, there's a crowd round your car waiting to assassinate you."

Thus, six months after her triumphant return from exile, Olga Chernov was plunged into a life of fear and flight. With their three children, the Chernovs fled to Saratov on the River Volga, far enough, they thought, from the main centres of Bolshevik influence to afford them a safe hiding place. Inexorably, the revolution followed them. Three times they were forced to move and on one occasion were fortunate not to be among the fifty political detainees executed in Saratov in revenge for an assassination attempt on Lenin in Moscow. Olga mourned:

Many of our comrades were among the victims: Boris Averkiev – only son of an old socialist exiled to Siberia during the Tsar's reign . . . Zenaide Mourachkina, a mistress in a communal school. They had been arrested on quite unimportant charges and were about to be released when this dreadful affair happened.

The brutal dissolution of the Constituent Assembly had taught the Chernovs that ideals alone would not defeat the Bolsheviks. Their spirits rose, therefore, when news filtered through that former Assembly deputies had established a democratic government in Samara, calling itself the Government of the Constituent Assembly, and were trying to raise a people's army to defend it. The Volga area seemed the ideal place from which to fight back, for here:

The peasants would always be faithful to the Revolutionary-Socialist policy. Here liberty was a tradition and the militant members of the Party had always done propaganda work, even during the Tsar's regime. As the elections had shown, socialism was very popular in this district.

When Victor departed for Samara in the autumn of 1918, Olga remained behind in Saratov to nurse a sick child, confident that she would soon be able to follow. While her daughter's life hung in the balance, she forgot about politics. When her interest in the world around her revived, it was only to discover that the Samara democracy had been destroyed by the dictatorship of Admiral Kolchak. A month later the Bolsheviks captured the town.

Downhearted, Olga returned to Moscow, knowing nothing of the fate of her husband. He had, in fact, escaped, and himself sneaked into Moscow in search of her. He was able to provide a first-hand account of the moment when Kolchak's troops and their Czech allies invaded the offices of the Government of the Constituent Assembly:

A brawl ensued and one of the deputies was killed; the others were only saved by the intervention of the Czechoslovakian commander. Now my husband was particularly hated by the monarchists, so the Czechoslovakian commander, fearing that he would meet with a tragic end, took him under his protection and thus he escaped from the white fury. The other deputies were put in prison and, in spite of the promise made to the Czechs, were finally transferred to Omsk and massacred there in December.

In Moscow the furtive life of hide-and-seek continued. Unable to register as citizens, the Chernovs received no rations and survived by bartering possessions and clothing for food on the black market. One night in January 1919 the Cheka invaded their hiding place:

There came an imperative rapping at the door which woke us up with a start. The electricity was not working; my husband got hastily dressed in the dark, but could not find his hat or his leather jacket, a sort of communist uniform in which he used to disguise himself. He jumped out of the window in his shirt-sleeves; it was twenty degrees below zero outside. Our room-mate lent us a fur cap and, having found the leather jacket, I threw them both out of the window after him. He still would not go away, but stood there outside the window asking for the manuscript of the "History of the Revolution" on which he was working.

On this occasion the Chernovs escaped arrest; an innocent neighbouring family of the same name were mistakenly apprehended instead. A fortnight later, however, a second raid led to the detention of Olga and her daughters, while Victor escaped again; he was never caught. Olga was interrogated by Latzis, one of the most feared of the Cheka agents. She remembered him as:

exactly like his portraits; a fairly young face with a large carefully trimmed beard, eyes that shone like ice, a cold impenetrable expression, and long white hands with polished fingernails. He wore a heavy diamond ring.

At first, she refused to reveal her true identity; in retaliation, the conditions of imprisonment

30 A street-search by Red Guard. At the height of the Terror few Soviet citizens were completely free from suspicion. (From *Engravings of the Great War,* by H.W. Wilson, published in 1919.)

were made so harsh that the children suffered fainting fits and hallucinations brought on by hunger. Finally, Olga agreed to sign a declaration to the effect that she was the wife of the "counter-revolutionary", Victor Chernov, and her daughters were released.

Olga Chernov herself did not get out until the autumn of 1922. During that three and a half years she was moved from prison to prison, and the conditions under which she was held varied with the political climate. In 1919, at the height of the Red Terror, she occupied a cell in a Cheka prison, from which inmates were daily led away to execution. Her cell-mate was a half-mad countess, who had been blackmailed by the Cheka into trying to trap Olga into revealing her husband's whereabouts. In the milder political climate of 1921-2 she was transferred to a section of Moscow's Boutiirky gaol which was reserved for political prisoners. Here the regime was relatively relaxed; the prisoners mingled freely with each other, produced a news-sheet and were able to organize amateur theatricals. However, when the Socialist Revolutionary group received word that party comrades were being mistreated in other prisons, they went on hunger strike. The punishment for this was several months' strict detention in isolated cells at the ancient prison of Yaroslav, where the daily ration was "a quarter of a pound of black bread and a plate of clear soup with rotten fish-heads in it".

In the prisons of the Cheka people could be found from all walks of life, who had fallen foul of the authorities. Boutiirky, for example, contained not only active political dissidents, but also many whose class origins or profession made them automatically suspect. There were:

Socialists, anarchists, constitutional democrats, monarchists; every kind of profession was represented too; lawyers, doctors, teachers, artists, clergymen and people connected with foreign embassies; there were also numerous princes, princesses, counts, one-time ministers and functionaries of high standing.

As the civil war drew to a close, Yaroslav prison filled up with captured "Greens", including, for a time, the celebrated guerilla leader, Ermolaev. The history of some prisoners was tragic. Olga made friends with a left-wing Socialist Revolutionary who had been imprisoned and tortured by the Whites in Kiev. After she was set free she returned to Moscow, where she continued to fight against the Bolsheviks, and was imprisoned by them. Most harrowing of all, however, were the fates of ordinary, non-political men and women threatened with death for what seemed to them a trivial offence or for no clear reason at all. Olga was sent one night to comfort an hysterical young peasant woman who had bought a piece of cloth on the black market and had been reported by a spy. When she was collected for execution, she was too terrified to walk and had to be dragged between two wardresses.

In October 1921 Olga Chernov was released without explanation, reunited with her daughters who had spent the past three years in Soviet orphanages, and expelled from the Soviet Union. While she prepared the necessary passports, she lived in an agony of suspense; the day before her scheduled departure her rooms were raided by the Cheka in search of compromising documents; they unpacked all the suitcases, throwing books and clothes all over the floor. When Olga and her daughters went to the station:

There was no one there to see us off; since my release I had become a dangerous person and none of my friends dared risk being seen with us. We left the city we loved so much like strangers.

In Estonia she was reunited with her husband. In spite of everything, both were confident that the fight for a democratic and socialist Russia was far from over and that one day they would be able to return. In fact, their reunion was the start of a life-long exile in France and the United States, and the Chernovs could only listen helplessly as the news leaked out of Russia of the sentences of death or life imprisonment inflicted on colleagues and friends they had left behind.

Frank McCullagh

Captain McCullagh of the Royal Irish Fusilliers was a member of the British Military Mission attached, in an advisory capacity, to the Kolchak regime at Omsk. When the capture of that town by the Red Army seemed imminent in November 1919, McCullagh and fourteen colleagues were detailed to stay behind when the rest of the British contingent moved out, to evacuate as many Russian civilians as possible.

In charge of a trainload of women and old people, McCullagh and his men left Omsk the day before its fall, and so began a gruelling two-month-long trek eastwards towards Vladivostok, in temperatures as low as forty-nine degrees below zero and surrounded by the chaos of a demoralized and defeated army. The volume of traffic moving in one direction had all but paralysed the Trans-Siberian railway; the British found that:

The obstacles we encountered during that long race were of the most varied and formidable description. In the first place, the track soon became blocked by an interminable ribbon of trains which moved very slowly and made prolonged and frequent halts. In the second place, we found great difficulty in getting water and fuel for our engine owing to the fact that there was no firewood at the stations and that

32 Admiral Kolchak (centre), Supreme Commander of the White forces in Siberia, reviewing troops in Omsk in September 1919, two months before its capture by the Red Army.

nearly all the water towers had run dry or got frozen. (*A Prisoner of the Reds,* London, 1922)

Moreover, many engine-drivers were Bolshevik sympathizers, and it was not unusual for them deliberately to allow an engine to "go cold" and seize up; during stoppages, the British party kept a guard on their driver day and night. In these circumstances, the law of the jungle prevailed; at each station:

The commandants of all the trains contended furiously all night long in the station master's office, not only for the privilege of being watered first, but also for the privilege of being put first on the west track, which was comparatively free. . . . But sometimes it looked as if the contest would end in bloodshed, for all the commanders went to these incredible conferences armed to the teeth and accompanied by soldiers who might be described, without much exaggeration, as walking arsenals, for, in addition to rifles, bayonets, swords, daggers and revolvers, some of them even carried hand-grenades.

At Bolotnaya McCullagh's train was brought to a complete halt and the party took to sleighs. It proved no joy-ride. Those who fell off the sleighs and were not quickly picked up faced certain death. A Bolshevik war-correspondent who took part in the pursuit of

31 Summer of 1919 and Kolchak's army begins the long retreat eastwards.

the retreating Whites later told McCullagh that thousands of frozen corpses had been found along the route. By night the sleigh-party sheltered in peasant huts among some of the silent victims of the Siberian civil war:

whose houses were thus filled every night by endless relays of armed men who ate up all the food; used up all the fuel; took away all the fodder, sleighs, horses and cattle; and frequently compelled all the men and boys to accompany them. When Kolchak's armies afterwards went to pieces at Krasnoyarsk, they left behind them, like spars and wreckage marking the spot where they had gone down, thousands of these unfortunate peasants, their horses lost, their sleighs smashed, themselves without any money or food or any means of getting back to their homes . . . districts, large as England, where there were formerly villages and cultivated fields, have now been reduced to the condition of deserts and are quite uninhabited.

At Krasnoyarsk the Red Army finally caught up with the convoy. Although he later became convinced that Bolshevism was a great evil, McCullagh was initially impressed by the discipline, courtesy and high morale of the troops, who, much to everyone's surprise, concentrated on winning as many converts to Communism as possible. No massacres took place; instead, there was a wholesale recruitment of former White soldiers into the Red Army. During the first week that McCullagh spent as a prisoner-of-war at Krasnoyarsk, twenty generals, one hundred and seventy-five staff officers and over four thousand other officers registered at the Red commandant's office, while twenty-four thousand ordinary soldiers were simply drafted into the Red Army with minimal formalities. The results bordered on the comical, for the higher-ranking officers were:

promptly reduced to the ranks, formed into awkward squads and drilled by a red corporal in the barrack square. . . . About two hundred white officers refused to serve in the Red Army and were consequently sent to work as convicts in the Ural mines. For these brave men I was

sincerely sorry, but I cannot honestly say that I was moved to tears by the spectacle of lazy and corrupt old generals . . . being made to do an honest stroke of work, probably for the first time in their lives.

Service under Kolchak had taught McCullagh that the Russian middle class lacked "backbone" and he thoroughly approved of the Bolshevik insistence that everyone should do some manual labour, noting with approval that Trotsky and his staff took their daily exercise by shovelling snow off the railway lines.

There was, however, much about Bolshevism that McCullagh found simply incomprehensible. When he asked to be repatriated, for example, he was taken aback by the local commissar's insistence that he first join the Communist Party:

The general Bolshevik view seemed to be that since open war was raging in England, as it was raging everywhere else throughout the world from China to Peru, between the capitalists and the proletariat, we could not be allowed to return home unless we gave satisfactory assurances that we were going back to take the side of the proletariat in that great struggle. It would be an act of treachery towards the British working class, now on the very point of sweeping away an effete parliamentary system, to let loose on them . . . paid assassins like us, hirelings of capitalism. And the only assurance that could be considered satisfactory would be our joining the communist party.

Before enlisting in 1914, McCullagh had been a journalist, and when all foreigners in Siberia were ordered to register with the authorities, he saw a chance of escape. He changed his uniform for civilian clothes and signed on as a foreign war-correspondent, while a stray British soldier took his place among the British prisoners and ensured that the number held by the Reds remained constant and no one noticed that he was missing – a ruse that could only have been successful in the chaos that was Russia in 1920. As a civilian he wrangled a pass to visit

Ekaterinburg, where he had been stationed in the spring of 1919, and was immediately struck by how much the town had changed. Under Kolchak:

it had been a very busy place . . . the station platform being a favourite place of assignation and always crowded with officers and ladies; the streets filled with soldiers, horses, cabs and the swift motor cars of great brass generals . . . the market place crowded with farmers' carts. In fact it was like any other army base, a town of good cheer, overcrowding, khaki, hastle, horses and sin.

Bolshevik Ekaterinburg, on the other hand, was much more "puritanical". A local official showed McCullagh round and boasted:

There is the restaurant where Kolchak's officers used to drink; it is now a school. . . . There is a villa which an old general presented to the Tsar; it is now an orphanage. A wealthy mineowner lived here; it is now a barrack.

McCullagh wheedled his way into a meeting of the local soviet, where:

I sat in my peasant's sheepskin coat at the reporters' table, and tried, with a success so great as to be almost disquieting, to look as plebeian as possible.

What he saw gravely disturbed him. Although the Bolsheviks were trying to rule Siberia by kindness and persuasion rather than by force, they were equally determined that not the least hint of organized opposition should arise in the soviets, and the supposedly democratic elections were, in fact:

a farce. To put the case in a nutshell, the ruling clique named its candidates and nobody dared to oppose them for fear of being a marked man.

The drift to dictatorship was also apparent when Trotsky visited Ekaterinburg in February 1920 as part of his campaign to convert the Red Army into labour battalions. The War Commissar founded a local

33 Leon Trotsky provided the Red Army with dynamic leadership and converted it into a formidable fighting force.

newspaper, *The Red Tocsin*, which shocked McCullagh by the way in which it sought to mould public opinion "by giving the public what they consider good for it and depriving it of all possibility of getting anything else". Likewise, while the Englishman could not but admire the simplicity of Trotsky's lifestyle, his prodigious workrate and the decisiveness with which he organized anti-typhus measures, he found Bolshevik methods of administration deplorable, for:

Just as Peter the Great used to have his boyars [nobles] forcibly shaved, so the Bolsheviks, when they started their great cleanliness and anti-typhus campaign in Ekaterinburg, used to seize grown men, shave them, cut their hair and subject them to a compulsory bath.

By the end of March McCullagh was convinced that the dangers Bolshevism presented to civilization far outweighed its virtues, and an illicit stay in Moscow confirmed his fears. Arrested by the Cheka on suspicion of living under a false identity, he managed to convince his captors that he was a bona fide journalist and was even offered a permanent job with a Soviet news agency. Afraid that he would be expected to write propaganda for distribution abroad, he politely declined and was granted permission to leave Russia with a party of British refugees whose evacuation had just been arranged. In May 1920 he boarded the British destroyer *Dongola* and, with infinite relief, relaxed back into a familiar world.

THE IMPACT ABROAD

To Russia's allies in the Great War must go at least part of the blame for the downfall of the Provisional Government. Obsessed with the German threat, few western politicians ever grasped the problems that continued participation in the war created for the young democracy. In May-June 1917, for example, the French socialist Minister of Munitions, Albert Thomas, spent a frantic month trying to persuade the Russians to launch a major offensive aimed at relieving pressure on the western front. Louis de Robien, a diplomat at the French embassy in Petrograd, viewed this mission with great scepticism; western observers who believed that the Russian people had overthrown the Tsar so that they might fight more effectively for an Allied victory were, in his opinion, "a lot of simpletons and are letting themselves in for bitter disappointments" (Louis de Robien, *The Diary of a Diplomat in Russia 1917-1918*, London, 1969). He was right. The offensive, duly launched in July, was a catastrophic failure and hastened the downfall of the Kerensky government; the last remnants of morale at the front totally dissipated and the troops became ever more receptive to Bolshevik promises of an early end to the war.

Allied policy after November 1917 was equally ill-thought-out. Hoping desperately that the overthrow of the Bolsheviks would herald Russia's return to the war, Britain, France and the USA distributed aid and encouragement indiscriminately to many of the White movements that sprang up in the border regions. When the rationale for this policy disappeared, with the armistice on the western front, these protégés could not simply be abandoned; "recent events," wrote British Foreign Secretary, Arthur Balfour, in February 1919, "have created obligations which last beyond the occasions which gave them birth." War-weariness, labour unrest and bankruptcy, however, made it impossible to send men and supplies on a scale large enough to be decisive. For example, the British sent to Siberia only the Middlesex Regiment, which had been declared unfit for active service. It was optimistically assumed that their mere presence would inspire the creation of popular, anti-Bolshevik armies, and when this failed to happen, Allied aid was doomed to ineffectiveness. The picture painted by Soviet historians of a calculated western attempt to restore the power of the landowners and factory bosses is very largely a myth.

Allied aid may have been of little assistance to the Whites, but it certainly provided the Bolsheviks with an important propaganda weapon, for they received no foreign aid and hence could now project themselves as the only truly patriotic Russians. It was also a significant (although by no means the only) cause of the profound distrust of western intentions that has survived to the present day. In 1918 the United States sent seven thousand troops to Siberia, mainly to guard against the Japanese taking advantage of the chaos there and making territorial gains. Of this incident the historians, S.E. Morison and H.S. Commager wrote:

Americans forgot the intervention, but the Bolsheviks did not. What it meant to them was that the United States had joined the capitalist countries of the Old World in an attempt to destroy them at a time when they were struggling for their life. (S.E. Morison and H.S. Commager, *The Birth of the American Republic*, vol. II, Oxford University Press, 1962)

For some the moral choice was clear-cut. Robien, for example, was convinced from the beginning that the February Revolution spelled disaster for his class. On 12 April 1917 he wrote in his diary:

Soon, the rabble will rule everywhere. It is fair punishment for the so-called "orderly people", who used their power solely in order to make war. They will learn, at the expense of their pocket books, that it would have been better to agree with their equals, even on the other side of the frontier, than all to be devoured by the internal enemy.

Winston Churchill, Secretary of State for War, waged a one-man campaign aimed at persuading the British government to launch an all-out crusade against "this nest of vipers", for:

between them and such order of civilisation as we have been able to build up since the dawn of history there can, as Lenin rightly proclaims, be neither truce nor pact. (W. Churchill, *The World Crisis: The Aftermath*, London, 1929)

For socialists and labour leaders the Bolshevik coup posed a dilemma. Many, who began as sympathizers, were irrevocably alienated by the terror and repression. Others, however, thrilled by the heroic struggle of the Russian proletariat against unequal odds and attracted by Bolshevik promises of a brighter tomorrow, were prepared to accept such methods as temporary aberrations. In 1920 a delegation of British socialists visited the Soviet Union. Among its members were Bertrand Russell and Clifford Allen; both men had been pacifists during the Great War and a close friendship had grown out of their common suffering. Over Russia, however, they quarrelled bitterly. Allen was optimistic. "I have come back", he wrote:

with numerous criticisms of what I have seen, yet I remain a convinced Communist. . . . I may say at the outset that I believe the world has more to learn from the Russian experiment than from any other social achievement in history. The tragedy of it all lies in the fact that such a remarkable experiment should have been worked out in face of such innumerable difficulties. Many critics have isolated what they have seen from the Russian history of the past five years, and have pronounced judgements as if the Communism at present practised in Russia exactly represented the Communist system as it must always be. (Quoted in A. Marwick, *Clifford Allen: The Open Conspirator,* London, 1964)

Russell, however, believed that the harsh and crude methods adopted by the Bolsheviks during the civil war could never be successfully translated into "a stable or desirable form of communism". A Bolshevik victory was more likely to be accompanied by "a complete loss of their ideals". All over the western world socialist parties split irreconcilably into Communist and democratic factions.

The Bolsheviks themselves expected their revolution to be the "torch to start the fires of revolution in the industrial countries of western Europe" (Lenin, *Letters from Switzerland*, 1917). Indeed, they had long assumed that Communism would not long survive in Russia unless it spread rapidly to the more advanced nations of the continent. Trotsky's first act on becoming Commissar for Foreign Affairs in November 1917 was to issue an appeal to the "toiling peoples of Europe oppressed and bled white" to overthrow their capitalist governments and establish a "proletarian peace". In 1919 the Comintern (the Third Communist International) was established in Moscow to co-ordinate the activities of Communist parties abroad. Early Communist revolutions did break out in Berlin, Munich and Budapest in 1919, but were quickly suppressed, and until 1945 Soviet Russia remained the world's only Communist state.

David Francis (1859-1927)

At two o'clock in the morning on the 28th April 1916, with the grinding of brakes and the pushing of people towards the doors, the Stockholm express came to a halt at the Finland Station of Petrograd . . . it was dark and cold. I was alone except for my loyal coloured valet, Philip Jordan. I had never been in Russia before. I had never been an ambassador before. My knowledge of Russia up to the time of my appointment had been that of the average intelligent American citizen – unhappily slight and vague. (D. Francis, *Russia from the American Embassy,* New York, 1921)

Thus David Francis, newly-appointed United States ambassador to the Russian Empire, took up his post, stepping for the first time on to Russian soil at the very place where, exactly a year later, Lenin was to make his triumphant return after twelve years of exile. A former governor of Missouri and a successful businessman, Francis was a man of settled political views. Democracy on the American model he regarded as the best possible form of government, while Germany posed a serious threat to civilized values which convinced him that the United States should enter the war on the side of the Allies as soon as possible. While

34 A.D. Protopopov, Minister of the Interior, 1916-17. By early 1917 a succession of equally unpopular appointments had cost Tsar Nicholas II the support of all classes of the Russian population.

Francis soon developed a genuine attachment to Russia and her people, he never ceased to judge all that happened there in the light of these other preoccupations.

Although he could not openly criticize the government to which he was accredited, he obviously formed no high opinion of the Tsarist regime. When the unpopular and reactionary Sturmer was appointed Foreign Minister in August 1916, Francis wrote to United States Secretary of State, Robert Lansing:

There is no doubt whatever that the liberal or progressive element in Russia is greatly disappointed and chagrined at the removal of Sazanov and the appointment of Sturmer. . . . I do not think there will be a revolution immediately after the close of the war; that would be premature, but if the court party does not adopt a more liberal attitude by extending more privileges to the people and their representatives in the Duma, a revolution will take place before the lapse of even a few years.

His reception of the February Revolution was predictably enthusiastic, for:

This revolution is the practical realisation of that principle of government which we have championed and advocated – I mean government by the consent of the governed.

At the ambassador's instigation, the United States became the first nation to recognize the Provisional Government, extended credit amounting to 256 million dollars and sent a team of experienced engineers to reorganize the chaotic Russian railway system.

Although this enthusiasm was genuine, Francis was also keenly aware that the February Revolution brought the United States great advantages; it had:

a powerful influence in placing America in a

position to enter the war backed by a practically unanimous public opinion. There can be no doubt that there would have been serious opposition to our aligning ourselves with an absolute monarchy.

Throughout 1917 he encouraged the Provisional Government to maintain its commitments to the Allies and thus prevent Germany from concentrating all her troops on the western front. That Russia's internal tensions might be exacerbated by the continuation of an unpopular war, and that the failure of the young democracy might thereby be made more likely, does not seem to have occurred to him, although he received numerous reports from American consuls in the provinces, which graphically described the deepening social upheaval. In April Francis wrote to Lansing with an almost shocking disregard for the realities of the Russian situation:

It has been my effort, and in that effort there has been no cessation, to impress upon all the importance of a vigorous prosecution of the war and to subordinate thereto all questions as to the rights of races or the recognition of classes.

Right up until November, Francis did not think a successful Bolshevik revolution was likely; when he realized that Lenin's regime was more than a temporary phenomenon, his opposition was total. The coup itself and the forcible dissolution of the Constituent Assembly he regarded as flagrant violations of the Russian people's right to self-determination and a danger to the rest of the world, for:

Bolshevism prevailing in Russia would extend its baleful influence to other countries and become more of a menace than it is now, not only to organised governments but to society itself. Bolshevik doctrines destroy family relations, and if they predominate, they will mean a return to barbarism.

For months Francis hoped that the Russian people could be roused from their apathy to unite against dictatorship, as the American people had done before them. Before press censorship became absolute, he published an open letter in which he warned:

I have not lost faith in the ability of the Russian people to solve their own problems. On the contrary, I believe that your patriotism, your pride, your sense of right and your love of justice will remove the difficulties that beset your pathway. But the time you have therefor is extremely limited. A powerful enemy is at your gates. . . . Your liberties are threatened.

In March 1918, when the other Allied ambassadors, fearing that they would be held as hostages, planned to leave the country, he expressed his determination to stay on, so that:

If any section of Russia refuses to recognise the authority of the Bolshevik government . . . I shall endeavour to locate that section and encourage the rebellion.

When Allied troops, including two thousand United States marines, landed at Archangel to guard stores of military equipment against a rumoured German encroachment, Francis set up his headquarters there and encouraged the Socialist Revolutionary, Chaikovsky, in his attempt to establish an anti-Bolshevik regime. The Archangel democracy proved a total failure. The hoped-for volunteer army of

35 American troops enter Archangel, 1918.

36 A Soviet view of Allied intervention from a Russian magazine in 1919: Denikin, Kolchak and Yudenitch are portrayed as dogs performing at the whim of the United States. The truth was more complex.

Republic and was now a fugitive living under the assumed name of Titov.

In October 1918 ill-health finally forced Francis to leave Archangel for treatment in a London hospital. He was never to return but his interest in Russian affairs did not waver. He roundly condemned those who advocated leaving Russia "to stew in her own juice". For him Russia was:

The chief victim of the world war. We owe her a debt which gratitude should prompt us to discharge. But beyond that, if we could but realise it, we owe it to ourselves, if we would preserve our institutions, to eradicate this foul monster – Bolshevism – branch, trunk and root. We owe it to society. We owe it to humanity, if we would save society from barbarism and humanity from slaughter.

freedom-loving peasants never materialized; monarchist officers kidnapped the ministers, while the British General Poole connived in the plot, claiming that he had "lost patience with the [Russians'] inability to govern themselves". Only the forceful protests of the other Allied commanders brought about the restoration of the democrats, but it soon became obvious that their faith in the democratic instincts of the Russian people was misplaced. Francis grew depressed, and his mood was not lightened by a visit from Tereschenko, who for a brief period in 1917 had been Foreign Minister of the Russian

Throughout 1919 he pestered President Wilson to send fifty thousand American soldiers to Petrograd to drive out the Bolsheviks and create the conditions in which the Russian people could "hold a free election . . . to a constituent assembly, that assembly to choose the form of government preferred by the majority of the Russian people". In the current atmosphere of war-weariness such a scheme stood no chance of acceptance, and it is difficult not to see this continued faith in Russian democracy as one more misjudgement by a man who saw Russia through American eyes.

Major H.N.H. Williamson (1886-   )

Educated at Eton and a graduate of the Royal Military Academy, Woolwich, Major Williamson had no doubts that Bolshevism was an unmitigated evil, which must be eradicated at all costs. Therefore, after four years' distinguished service in France, for

which he had been awarded the Military Cross and the Belgian Croix de Guerre, he volunteered for duty with the British Military Mission in South Russia, whose function was to advise and distribute supplies to the armies of General Denikin. His motives were simple:

I offered myself in a spirit of adventure and of preservation of the traditional ethics of the caste to which I belonged. I had no more time for mutinous soldiers and sailors who ill-treated and massacred their officers than I had for political adventurers from the criminal classes who murdered their Tsar and his helpless family. I came from a group whose privileges in those days were very real, and I saw the Russian Revolution not so much as a fight by workers to put right a lot of wrongs as a struggle by evil people to do away with the society to which I belonged. (*A Farewell to the Don,* London, 1970)

Williamson arrived in Ekaterinodar, the headquarters of the White armies, in April 1919, when White fortunes were on the upturn. He remained with them as an artillery instructor until the final evacuation of southern Russia in February 1920 and observed at close quarters the strengths and weaknesses of the anti-Bolshevik movement. During this period he kept a detailed diary of his day-to-day impressions, which, fifty years later, was edited and published.

Williamson's first contacts in Russia, the staff officers of Ekaterinodar, made a poor impression:

37 British sailors march through Vladivostok, 1918. Williamson's experiences in South Russia taught him that Allied aid to the Whites was often grudging and ineffective.

For the most part they knew nothing at all about what was going on. If they did, they gave only vague answers and, when pressed, took refuge behind the language barriers. Mostly they were kind-hearted and generous to the point of absurdity but, apart from swearing frightful oaths of revenge on the Bolsheviks, they were not much use. They were lazy, arrogant, ignorant and often cowardly.

This initial judgement was confirmed by contact with the frontline troops. At the battle for Constantinograd, a small town near Poltava, Major Williamson and his commanding officer, General Holman, encountered a machine-gun crew who had jammed their guns. The following scene ensued:

Holman looked at me: "Can't we fix this?" he asked.
"I think so, Sir."
"Let's try."
We took off our coats and got two of the three guns into action again, while all ranks of the Russians looked on from behind in amazement. "A general!" I heard them saying. "A general who knows how to put a gun right himself and doesn't mind doing it."

It was difficult for any outsider to avoid the conclusion that the White officer corps was responsible for much of the demoralization that afflicted the White armies. The common soldiers, Williamson concluded:

were patient, good-humoured and hard-working, but they were largely despised by their officers and treated abominably. It took a great deal to discourage them but their officers *did* discourage them and they deserted constantly in ones and twos and groups; and, sometimes even, when attacks were pressed by shouting staff officers on excited horses, they simply rose up en masse, murdered their officers and walked over to the enemy.

None of this dimmed Williamson's belief in the essential rightness of the White cause. The sufferings of soldiers and civilians, even when

39 Williamson and his companions regarded the Bolsheviks as the embodiment of cruelty and oppression. In fact, atrocities were shared fairly equally between both sides, as the fate of these Red Army soldiers, captured by Denikin's troops in 1919, clearly shows.

38 General A.I. Denikin inspecting a British-trained and equipped tank corps, October 1919.

exacerbated by their own incompetence, and the numerous stories of Bolshevik atrocities only stiffened his emotional attachment to a class threatened by "a semi-criminal, semi-educated, self-seeking class of political agitators". When other British officers poured scorn on the Whites, Williamson argued that:

it was the worst possible form to criticise a people who had suffered so severely, and I managed to avoid seeing some of the worst excesses. I just didn't want to see them, in fact. I was already greatly attached to the Don Cossacks and preferred not to look . . .

He was not the only volunteer who felt so intensely. Angus Campbell, heir to a Scottish dukedom, who acted for a while as Williamson's interpreter, was invalided out suffering from typhus. Within six months he was back, this time as a civilian, "in the hope of being of some further use to the people whose cause he had so loyally taken up".

Such enthusiasts were disgusted and embarrassed by the lukewarmness of official British policy, which Williamson considered to be criminally short-sighted. The civil war was not purely a Russian concern; the Whites should be seen as a "bulwark against the fast-flowing tide of communism which was already surging from eastern Europe into the West". If the Allies had grasped this at the beginning and been:

wholehearted about their anti-communism and had sent sufficient troops in the early days, they could have walked into Moscow, because at that time the Reds were as demoralised as the Whites and a few battle-trained regiments could have cut through the defences like a knife through butter.

The belated help that did finally arrive was, in Williamson's opinion, equally ill-conceived; the British determination to "let Russia work out her own salvation" (Williamson), which was carried out to the last letter of the law, "very nearly wrecked everything in the early summer of 1919". Williamson's artillery team, for example, had:

no authority to interfere in the appalling muddle that existed, even though we saw our good equipment rotting in the goods yards, or spoiled and wasted by the inexperienced and never over-energetic Russian officers at the bases.

By November 1919 the White armies had retreated to Novocherkassk, capital of the Don Cossacks, and it was here that Williamson was stationed when the news arrived that Britain was withdrawing all aid from the faltering Whites. Thereafter he received from the younger officers "many angry looks and muttered insults which, after an evening's vodka, they took precious little pains to conceal". Understandably, he found it particularly:

hurtful and humiliating, and the thing that hurt me most when trying to reconcile myself to the rapidly lowering barometer of British prestige, was that, despite all our efforts to explain in letters home how very much more than a family quarrel between Russians was at issue, the ground was deliberately pulled from under our feet by politicians whose knowledge of the subject did not go far enough to know that Kharkov was a town and not a general.

When the British Mission withdrew, Williamson remained behind to share the last tragic months of Denikin's regime. The Cossack General Sidorin, to whom he was attached, abandoned him and left him to make his own evacuation plans, while all around him the White armies fell to pieces. On the retreat from Novocherkassk, General Janov:

took no steps to adopt a fighting or protective formation and the column wound unguarded across the endless snow that was broken only here or there by a dark patch of pine forest, the men with their heads down and huddled in their saddles, indifferent to what happened to them.

In the rear, staff officers continued their

accustomed irresponsible behaviour. Some were:

still busily engaged in exchanging and selling loot, and those employed in equipment stores had enormous sums of money. There had even been an outbreak of debauchery and gambling and some highly-placed officers were involved. All this, while wounded officers were hanging themselves and refugees — mostly officers' families — were dying of cold and hunger in the trains into which they had piled.

As soldiers and civilians fled before the Red Army to Novorosissk, the last Black Sea port open to the Whites, Green Guards preyed upon the refugee trains, "murdering and robbing, even tearing the clothes from the backs of the passengers and flinging them out into the snow to freeze to death"· At Novorosissk itself there were only enough ships to evacuate a fraction of those who wanted to go, and hysteria set in as people realized that they would be left behind to face the Red Army. Williamson watched the scene on the quayside:

Troops were throwing away their shoulder straps and officers were tearing off their epaulettes because the Reds had an obsession about the symbols of privilege . . ., others shot themselves in despair, whilst fat merchants offered suitcases full of paper roubles for the chance of a passage. Young girls were desperately trying to get themselves married to Englishmen — not for love but to get out of the country as British subjects — and several actually did, making arrangements to part as soon as they were in safety.

When he finally dragged himself away from the waterfront, "my head was bursting, my joints shaking and I felt rotten in body and rotten in heart". He was, in fact, incubating typhus, but his spiritual despair went even deeper. The Russian adventure, which had started with such high hopes, had been:

one long list of failures, which became more complete and more irredeemable the more I looked at it. My work had ended in failure too, failure in ideals, failure in execution. And what would history say of the failure of the British Mission to South Russia and of the inefficiency of most of its members?

Mentally reliving these events fifty years later, Brigadier Williamson (as he had since become) had no regrets about what he had done but wondered whether the cause had been worth it. He might, he realized, have "attached ideals to certain subjects which may not have deserved it".

George Lansbury (1859-1940)

For George Lansbury, prominent member of the British Independent Labour Party (ILP) and editor of the *Daily Herald*, the Russian Revolution might have created a crisis of conscience. Throughout most of his political career, which began in local politics in London's East End in the 1880s, he had followed a creed in which socialism, pacifism, democracy and Christianity were combined and which led him to condemn both the "imperialist" war of 1914-18 and the concept of violent revolution. Surprisingly, when he visited the Soviet Union in February 1920, he did not find it difficult to embrace Bolshevik Russia as the first living embodiment of his principles, the "dawn" which would lead to the "full noonday sunshine of the new day". He concluded early on that:

No set of men and women responsible for a revolution of the magnitude of the Russian Revolution ever made fewer mistakes or carried their revolution through with less interference with the rights of individuals, or with less terrorism and destruction, than the men in control in Russia. When I speak of the rights of individuals I exclude property rights, for one object of the revolution was to abolish for good and all the "right" of one set of individuals to exploit the life and work of their fellow men and women. (*What I Saw in Russia*, London, 1920)

He interviewed Bolshevik leaders and was filled with admiration for their personal qualities. Lenin, he concluded, was no lover of violence and butchery for its own sake, and in this Lansbury was probably right. He welcomed the spirit of equality and comradeship that characterized social and political relationships. The first Russians he met, the soldiers who escorted him across the frontier from Finland, seemed to embody the virtues of the new order:

So far as I could judge, the relationships between officers and men were extremely

40 George Lansbury (second from left) and his family, 1923.

cordial. There is no "kow-towing" as in our army; no clicking of heels and saluting for the special benefit of officers. . . . We all sat at the same table for our food and throughout there was a true spirit of comradeship among us.

Such observations were valid enough, but Lansbury allowed his optimistic view of human nature and his own psychological need to see hope for mankind in the victory of Bolshevism to warp his judgement, and he drew conclusions about the future development of the Soviet Union that a less emotional, less involved observer might have shunned.

Only civil war and foreign intervention, argued Lansbury, prevented the full flowering of political and industrial democracy in Russia. The "Extraordinary Commission" (Cheka), for example, was a necessary concomitant of British and French assistance to the Whites, for:

the conditions may justify even a socialist revolutionary government in using means it despises to safeguard itself and the revolution entrusted to its care.

From here to the conclusion that "when peace is established the Secret Police will be abolished" was a relatively easy step. That there might be those in Russia who opposed Bolshevism for its own sake and were not in the pay of foreign powers, Lansbury hardly considered. If he had done so, he might have given thought to the danger that political oppression would become a permanent feature of the Soviet system.

The British socialist visited a model workshop organized by Russian craftsmen who had spent years of exile in the United States and who had only recently returned home. He was greatly impressed by the spectacle of industrial democracy in action:

The managers are elected by the workers on the principle one person one vote; all real grievances are settled by the vote of all; rules and regulations are discussed and approved. All deferred to expert opinion on matters requiring special knowledge, but each worker was expected and encouraged to make suggestions as to how to increase output and at the same time to reduce exhausting labour to a minimum.

Lansbury was realist enough to admit that such factories were exceptional and that "there is at present very much central control", but he was naively convinced that worker-control would soon become the norm. In the same optimistic spirit, he believed implicitly that Trotsky's labour armies, which were then in the first stages of formation, were the key to the rebuilding of the Russian economy, and that peasant attachment to Communist principles was developing rapidly. An impartial examination of what was to happen in Russia in 1920 and 1921 indicates that Lansbury's judgement was emotional rather than realistic.

Given these optimistic prognostications, there was little difficulty in reconciling Bolshevism and Christianity. In spite of his professed atheism, Lenin:

typifies in my judgement a living expression of

41 F.E. Dzerzhinsky, fanatical and austere head of the Cheka.

the words of Tom Paine [an eighteenth-century political theorist]: "The world is my country, to do good is my religion, all mankind are my brethren". . . his whole life seems to be that of one of the saints of old.

The liberal soviet laws on marriage and divorce, which encouraged civil marriage and easy divorce and which outraged many western Christians, seemed to Lansbury a victory of humanitarian Christianity over stale conventions.

However, Lansbury's account of his visit, published in London in June 1920, had its own peculiar value in the context of that year. The powerful anti-Bolshevik lobby in Britain and France was equally guilty of interpreting events in Russia to suit its own political purposes, and Lansbury consciously set out to provide a corrective to the one-sided picture of Bolshevik barbarity to which the public were exposed. He made some shrewd observations. The press, for example, constantly castigated the Bolsheviks for imprisoning foreign nationals on suspicion of spying. Yet in Britain during the war:

They [the press] have supported every infraction of liberty by the government. They have hounded the government on to "intern them all"; to pass laws that make it impossible for many foreigners to set foot in this country, and these are the people who denounce the Bolsheviks for putting political offenders and aliens in prison.

Likewise, the capitalist press wrote gleefully of privations in Russia and attributed them to the abolition of private enterprise. To Lansbury, however, these were two separate issues. It was true that private shops and businesses had been closed but that was no loss:

What has happened in Russia is just this; all the old useless forms of labour are, to a large extent, abolished. There is no advertising, no illicit adulteration, no opening of competitive shops and stores . . . the superfluous shops and stores which used to fleece the poor are also gone, and this is a fact for rejoicing rather than sorrowing.

In its place, a rational state system of production and distribution was springing up, that would ensure fair shares for all. If the standard of living was appallingly low, that was not an indictment of the new order but the responsibility of the Allied blockade; with peace there would be "abundance for everybody". Meanwhile, the British press pursued its prejudices and forgot:

The effect of this blockade which prevented medicines and anaesthetics going into Russia, which was seen when a British soldier was obliged to submit to an operation for the removal of his eye without an anaesthetic. Hundreds of thousands of Russians obliged to undergo operations were treated in the same manner.

Lansbury's enthusiasm for Soviet Russia created difficulties for the ILP, for on his

THE BEAR TURNS.

42 An anti-soviet cartoon from *Punch*, 4 June 1919. The strident anti-Bolshevik tone of the press convinced Lansbury that the British people were receiving a one-sided view of Russian affairs.

return he argued that membership of the Third International (Comintern) would not automatically commit his party to the principle of violent revolution. This assurance was based on the generally favourable impression he had brought back from Russia and on a conversation he had had with Lenin, in which the Soviet leader had remarked rather ambiguously:

You think you can accomplish the revolution without violence? I think you will not be able to do so. If in England you are able to do this, well and good. No one wants bloodshed for bloodshed's sake.

Fellow ILP leader, Ramsay MacDonald mocked Lansbury's gullibility:

What we are really driving at is this. We hope that Moscow will say for our benefit that it is not Moscow, that dictatorships are not dictatorships, revolution not revolution, and that in the Russian turmoil the English language as well as the bourgeoisie has been upset. (Quoted in D. Marquand, *Ramsay MacDonald,* London, 1977)

Nevertheless, an ILP delegation travelled to Moscow in April 1920, only to discover to their horror that membership of the Comintern was open only to parties of a "revolutionary temper". No section of the British Labour Party ever joined the Moscow organization, but the dilemma posed for democratic socialists by the existence of the Soviet Union, a dilemma that Lansbury evaded but his colleagues could not, haunted the labour movement for decades to come.

Emma Goldman (1869-1940)

Russian by birth, Emma Goldman had lived in the United States since the age of seventeen. In December 1919, aged fifty, she was deported, together with two hundred and forty-eight other unwanted foreign nationals, and arrived in Russia in January 1920, at the beginning of the last year of the civil war. As an anarchist, who had endured periods of imprisonment for her political activities, she had decided views on the course the revolution ought to take. True revolution, she believed, could only be made and maintained by genuine popular participation. If the will of the people were overridden by those who thought they knew what was best for society, the result would be the rise of a new tyranny as

43 Emma Goldman, 1934.

oppressive as the one that had been overthrown, for:

No revolution can be truly and permanently successful unless it puts its emphatic veto on all tyranny and centralisation, and determinedly strives to make the revolution a real revaluation of all economic, social and cultural values. Not mere substitution of one political party for another in control of the government . . . not the dictatorship of a new class over an old one, not political scene-shifting of any kind, but the complete reversal of all authoritarian principles will alone serve the revolution. (*My Disillusionment in Russia,* New York, 1923)

Although force might be needed to create this new society, injustice and arbitrary violence could never be excused, for:

no revolution can ever succeed as a factor of liberation unless the MEANS used to further it be identical in spirit with the PURPOSE to be achieved.

In 1917 the Bolsheviks had adopted the popular slogans "Bread", "Peace" and "Land" and Emma Goldman arrived in Petrograd convinced that the new government was the genuine voice of the people and intent on making Soviet Russia her new home. She spent the uncomfortable, month-long sea voyage from America "in a kind of trance":

I was bound for Russia and all else was almost blotted out. I would behold with mine own eyes matuushka Rossiya (Mother Russia), the land freed from economic and political masters; the Russian dubinushka, as the peasant was called, raised from the dust; the Russian worker, the modern Samson, who with a sweep of his mighty arm had pulled down the pillars of decaying society.

The deportees were cordially received and Zorin, a senior Communist official, was delegated to look after them. Emma was eager to be reunited with Bill Shatov, an American who had been in Russia since 1917, and was mystified because the telegram she had sent

him from Finland had not been answered. Shatov, Zorin reassured her, was in Siberia, running the railway system there. A few days later, however, Emma met, by accident, Shatov's sister-in-law, who took her home:

When we reached their apartment I found myself embraced by big jovial Bill himself. How strange of Zorin to tell me that Shatov had left for Siberia! What did it mean? Shatov explained that he had been ordered not to meet us at the border, to prevent his giving us our first impressions of Soviet Russia. He had fallen into disfavour with the government and was being sent to Siberia into virtual exile. His trip had been delayed and therefore we still happened to find him.

The first seeds of doubt had been sown.

For six months Emma lived in Petrograd and Moscow and was daily confronted with evidence that the revolution fell far short of her dreams. Fellow anarchists regaled her with stories about the silencing and imprisonment of socialists who did not see eye-to-eye with the Bolsheviks. At first, she refused to listen, for:

everything in me cried out against this indictment. It sounded impossible; it could not be. Someone was surely at fault, but probably it was they, my comrades, I thought. They were unreasonable, impatient for immediate results. Was not violence inevitable in a revolution, and was it not imposed upon the Bolsheviks by the Interventionists? My comrades were indignant. "Disguise yourself so that the Bolsheviki do not recognise you; take a pamphlet of Kropotkin [a Russian anarchist] and try to distribute it in a Soviet meeting. You will soon see whether we told you the truth."

When a Menshevik was howled down at a meeting of the Petrograd Soviet, she was concerned enough to discuss the matter with Zorin. He only laughed and remarked that "free speech is a bourgeois superstition; during a revolutionary period there can be no free speech". Still Emma hesitated:

I was rather dubious about the sweeping

statement, but I felt that I had no right to judge. I was a newcomer, while the people at the Tauride Palace had sacrificed and suffered so much for the Revolution. I had no right to judge.

Emma had expected the standard of living in Soviet cities to be low, but the lack of comradely spirit shown by ordinary people came as something of a shock. On her first visit to Moscow, she observed that:

Everyone rushed about as a detached unit in quest of his own, pushing and knocking against everyone else. Repeatedly I saw women or children fall from exhaustion without anyone stopping to lend assistance. People stared at me when I would bend over the heap on the slippery pavement or gather up the bundles that had fallen into the street. I spoke to friends about what looked to me like a strange lack of fellow-feeling. They explained it as a result partly of the general distrust and suspicion created by the Cheka, and partly due to the absorbing task of getting the day's food. One had neither vitality nor feeling left to think of others.

She found it difficult to tolerate injustices done to individuals. In the spring of 1920, for example, she was asked to prepare quarters in Petrograd for a further one thousand Russian citizens due to be deported from the United States. As a work-force she was given "a one-armed old man, a consumptive woman and eight boys and girls, mere children, pale, starved and in rags"; these, she was informed, were convicted speculators. The prisoners themselves, however, told her a different story:

They were no speculators, they protested; they were starving, they had received no bread in two days. They were compelled to go out to the market to sell matches or thread to secure a little bread. In the midst of this scene the old man fainted from exhaustion, demonstrating better than words that he had speculated only in hunger.

Later in the year Emma Goldman went to work for the Museum of the Revolution in

44 A punishment detachment of the Red Army moves into a village, April 1921. The sympathies of foreign socialists were sometimes alienated by the prolonged oppressiveness of Bolshevik rule.

Petrograd and, as part of her duties, undertook a tour of the Ukraine and the Caucasus to collect exhibits from the revolutionary period in the provinces. Away from the capital, she would be able, she hoped, to mix more freely with the people and decide once and for all what she really felt about the Bolshevik regime. She found little to comfort her. After a tour of Kharkov prison she was haunted for days by the faces of the men and women in the condemned cells – "their eyes full of terror at the torturing uncertainty, fearing to be called at any moment to face death". Her guide, a local Communist Party official, shrugged it off with the comment, "We are living in a revolutionary period; these matters cannot be helped", but Emma could not be so cavalier; that innocent people, who had never plotted against the revolution, should be penalized merely because of their class or education struck her as a monstrous injustice. She was introduced to a young woman doctor who had been sent to work in a remote village. She and her husband were:

completely isolated from all intellectual life, having neither papers, books nor associates. Her husband would begin his rounds early in the morning and return late at night, while she had to attend to her baby and household, besides taking care of her own patients. She had only recently recovered from typhus and it was hard for her to chop wood, carry water, wash and cook and look after her sick. But what made their life unbearable was the general antagonism towards the intelligentsia. They had it constantly thrown up to them that they were bourgeois and counter-revolutionists, and they were often accused of sabotage.

By the time Emma returned to Petrograd in the autumn of 1920 she could no longer "close my eyes and ears" to the "blind errors and conscious crimes that were stifling the revolution". Her agony was all the greater because she felt compelled to keep silent:

How could I speak out when the country was still besieged on several fronts? It would mean working into the hands of Poland and Wrangel. For the first time in my life I refrained from exposing grave social evils. I felt as if I were betraying the trust of the masses, particularly of the American workers, whose faith I dearly cherished.

The struggle within the Communist Party over the future of the Russian trade unions was in full swing and all Emma's instinctive sympathies lay with the defeated Workers' Opposition. It was the Kronstadt Affair, however, that provoked the final breach. The demands of the sailors for freely-elected soviets, freedom of expression for all left-wing parties and an end to requisitioning from the peasants echoed Emma's own beliefs, and:

Kronstadt broke the last thread that held me to the Bolsheviki. The wanton slaughter they had instigated spoke more eloquently against them than aught else. Whatever their pretences in the past, the Bolsheviki now proved themselves the most pernicious enemies of the Revolution. I could have nothing further to do with them.

With no future left for her in the Soviet Union, but only after numerous bureaucratic delays, she left the country, never to return, in December 1921. It was just:

one year and eleven months since I had set foot on what I believed to be the promised land. My heart was heavy with the tragedy of Russia. One thought stood out in bold relief: I must raise my voice against the crime committed in the name of the Revolution. I would be heard regardless of friend or foe.

45 The Red Army crossing the ice to attack Kronstadt on the night of 17 March 1921.

THE AFTERMATH

In *State and Revolution*, written in 1917, Lenin argued that the future of Soviet Russia lay with the dictatorship of the proletariat and the evolution of "socialist democracy"; supreme power would rest with the working class and their peasant allies and be expressed through freely-elected soviets; all other classes would disappear. There was, however, to be no question of dictatorship by a minority; the masses were to assume full political, economic and military responsibility for their own future and would be aided in the task by the natural development of a collectivist morality, in which the individual would spontaneously sacrifice his personal interests for the common good. Conventional army discipline, for example, was to replaced by the "armed people", responsible for the election and dismissal of their own officers and for enforcing discipline upon themselves.

Although the civil war conveniently resulted in the death or exile of most of the old upper and middle classes, it also destroyed the dream of proletarian democracy and replaced, it with dictatorship by the Communist Party. Amongst a population in which politically-conscious workers were far outnumbered by apathetic peasants such an outcome was always likely, but the drift to minority dictatorship became inevitable when civil war

46 Child victims of starvation and civil war, Samara, 1922.

killed off the majority of dedicated working-class Communists and forced the Party to rely for support on the less politically-conscious sections of the working community. They could not be counted on to sacrifice present comfort in the interests of the future and had therefore to be controlled. The 1918 Constitution laid down that Russia was to be ruled by a hierarchy of freely-elected soviets, but by 1920 it was obvious even to a foreign observer like Captain McCullagh that the democratic process had been replaced by party coercion. Kamenev and Zinoviev, so often worsted in their disputes with Lenin, had come uncomfortably close to the mark when they had argued in October 1917 in Sukhanov's flat that a Bolshevik insurrection would be premature, as the masses were not yet politically mature enough to run a socialist system themselves.

If the Party was to wield absolute power, the quality of its membership would be crucial. With the decimation of the first generation of Communist activists, however, leadership fell increasingly into the hands of men who made a career out of party politics. Many were sincere and dedicated but, immersed in full-time political work, tended to lose touch with the reality of life on the factory floor. The less scrupulous saw Party membership as the key to a distinguished career and privileged lifestyle. It was a far cry from the ideal of popular self-administration, and Lenin's last years were haunted by the fear that the Soviet Union was falling into the hands of a new generation of bureaucrats.

Moreover, by 1921 it was clear that the regime would not be secure until it provided the peasantry with direct benefits. At the Tenth Congress of the Russian Communist

Party, Lenin introduced the New Economic Policy (N.E.P.), which restored to Russia some elements of a free market economy, and the next few years saw the re-emergence of the factory-owner and small businessman, the growth of a prosperous class of enterprising peasants (the Kulaks) and the appearance of the Nepmen, who grew rich from the profits to be made transferring goods from producer to customer.

Lenin saw the N.E.P. as a temporary retreat, a step taken backwards in order that greater strides might later be made forwards to a fully socialist economy. "You must first attempt," he argued, "to build small bridges which shall lead a land of small peasant holdings through State Capitalism to Socialism. Otherwise you will never lead tens of millions of people to Communism." Yet this argument, acceptable to sophisticated Party leaders, was hard for ordinary Communists to swallow; it seemed to many that they had sacrificed themselves only to bring undeserved privileges to non-Party specialists and grasping peasants. The Workers' Opposition faction, with its demand that the trade unions should run the factories, was an off-shoot of growing grass-roots discontent and a painful reminder of an earlier, more idealistic form of Communism. In the end, it only hastened the tightening of the dictatorship.

While the Party stranglehold over Russian political life increased in the years after 1917, discussion within the Party had remained remarkably free. Lenin had won the great debates of October 1917 and March 1918 through the force of his arguments, not because his opponents were afraid to answer back. As late as 1920 Zinoviev could still insist that "any comrade, if he considers it necessary to steer the Party and the Soviet ship in another direction, can speak up about this – this is his right". In the desperate situation of 1921, however, Lenin, supported by Trotsky, was grimly determined that the N.E.P. should be enforced regardless of the weight of Party opinion against it. The Tenth Party Congress made the fateful decision to ban factions within the Party on pain of immediate expulsion. Henceforth no Party member who wished to remain active in politics dared challenge the decisions of the leadership, power was concentrated in ever fewer hands and the way lay open to one-man dictatorship.

For White Russians defeat meant exile. For most, the first port of refuge was Constantinople, which by 1922 had so many Russian shops, cafes and churches that a homesick General Lukomsky sometimes almost believed that "the ancient Russian dream had come true and that Constantinople had become a Russian city". General Wrangel and the Grand Duke Nicholas Nicholaevitch, uncle of the last Tsar, founded the World Organization of Russian War Veterans (R.O.V.S.), intended as the nucleus of a new White army, but for the next twenty years hopes of a renewed war against the Communists remained but a dream. Some exiles built new careers; several colourful troupes of bare-back riders toured Europe between the wars and among their performers was at least one general – Shkuro. Others, without special skills or connections, survived in poverty, among them Makhno, who died in Paris in 1935. For some the shattering of their hopes proved too much to bear. The Menshevik Chkeidze, Chairman of the Petrograd Soviet in 1917 and President of the Independent Republic of Georgia until its occupation by the Bolsheviks in 1921, committed suicide in Paris in 1926, distressed at the total suppression of local culture and political life in his homeland by high-handed commissars from Moscow, whose power had gone unchecked since Lenin's death.

During the Second World War a final desperate attempt came to oust Soviet rule from Russia. Ukrainian and Cossack recruits fought alongside the German invaders and a senior Soviet commander, Vlasov, defected in 1942. All these hopes perished with the German surrender, however, and thousands of defectors were reluctantly shipped back to face execution or oblivion in Stalin's labour camps. Thus was played out the last act in the uncompromising battle for control of Russia, that had begun with such high hopes nearly thirty years before.

Elisaveta Fen

Elisaveta Fen was the youngest daughter of a family of minor landowners, and her father had been a provincial governor in Byelorussia before the war. A student in Petrograd at the time of the February Revolution, she had shared the hopes of many of her contemporaries that the autocracy would be replaced by a democratic government like those of western Europe. The Bolshevik regime she regarded with great distaste, condemning Lenin as the "man who had deliberately contrived the use of millions of human beings as guinea pigs in a gigantic laboratory", and her account of Soviet life immediately after the civil war was not, therefore, that of a sympathetic observer.

Elisaveta Fen was not a political person. Although Odessa, the city in which she was trapped by the civil war, changed hands five times between 1918 and 1921, she managed to avoid serious trouble with the authorities and ensured bodily survival by taking clerical jobs in Soviet offices, posts that entitled her to third-category rations. Her health, however, was seriously undermined by privation, especially the lack of protein. By 1921:

I used to wake up in the morning feeling as if I were about to die. The sensation of mental and physical nausea was so intense that I could hardly raise myself on my bed, and groaned at the prospect of putting on clothes which would come into contact with my boils. (*Remember Russia,* London, 1973)

In February 1923 she moved to Moscow. The New Economic Policy was then two years old and its effects were filtering through to the big cities. Food supplies were at last adequate for health, although rather monotonous; the restaurant Elisaveta patronized served a continual diet of minced-beef rissoles and macaroni, which "supplied the protein I had been starved of for so long". Dress materials and sweets were once again appearing in the shops. The legalization of private trade, combined with a massive consumer demand after almost a decade of chronic shortages, provided numerous opportunities for enterprising Russians to earn a good living. Elisaveta herself had been lured to Moscow by her old schoolfriend, Liolia, who had written glowing reports of life in the capital:

Her husband had opened a bookshop specialising in foreign languages and rare secondhand books. Her mother had set herself up as a successful seamstress. Liolia herself was taking private lessons in singing from a former teacher of the Moscow Conservatoire. Everything was going swimmingly.

The improvement in living conditions was only relative; life was still, in many ways, rather spartan. The public transport system, for example, had yet to recover completely from its total breakdown during the civil war. Moscow trams:

were few and far between, and when one came, packed to over-flowing, the crowd waiting at the stopping place would rush at it, jostling one another in their desperate eagerness to get in. But people were already clinging to the railings or the back door-steps. In the pushing and squeezing that followed the strongest usually got on and the weakest were left behind. Often one was forced to let several trams go by before one managed to get on one. But this did not mean that one could relax; once inside you had to work your way through to the front of the car, for one was not permitted to get off at the back. . . . A tram journey had become an athletic feat, a test of endurance and sometimes a risk to life and limb. It was certainly ruinous to clothes; one could easily lose most of one's coat buttons or have a sleeve torn off.

Personal luxuries were still so scarce that petty pilfering was endemic. At one time, small items kept disappearing from Elisaveta's room and she suspected that her neighbour's teenage daughter was the culprit:

One day it would be a reel of white cotton, another day a comb or a nailbrush. . . . Such small objects of personal use were still in such short supply that you could wait months to replace them.

Going for an interview for a job at the American Relief Administration, which was housed in a mansion built for a former sugar millionaire, she was awe-struck by the unaccustomed opulence:

One reads of the intense feelings, of the powerful impact ordinary things can produce on a prisoner who is released from his cell for the first time after months – or years – of captivity. My reactions to the interior of Morozov's house after years of unrelieved drabness and cramped conditions of living were something of that order. As I followed the page boy up the wide carpeted staircase and through a couple of lofty rooms with large windows overlooking a garden of great trees, I was seized with a longing to stay there, doing no matter what, having this space around me, this quietness and the view of the hoary trees outside my window.

Finding accommodation was a particular hardship, since Moscow was experiencing a population explosion as people returned after the civil war exodus from the towns. Elisaveta's first Moscow home was in Liolia's flat, where four people shared:

three small rooms and a kitchen, all but choked with indispensable pieces of furniture. A single bed and a sewing machine in Varvara Mihailovna's [Liolia's mother] room; a double bed and a grand piano in Liolia and Volodya's room (you could hardly squeeze past the bed to the piano stool); a dining table, some chairs, a dresser and a bed behind a screen in the dining room. I used to sleep in Varvara Mihailovna's room on an iron camp bed which could only be set up after the treadle machine had been folded up and moved out into the passage.

On Elisaveta's first night in the city, "Varvara Mihailovna had to finish a piece of sewing which was to be collected in the morning, before my bed could be made ready for me."

Party dictatorship and the N.E.P. were producing new privileged classes. The drive for industrial efficiency had brought back into favour those members of the old middle class who had industrial expertise. When she left Liolia's flat, Elisaveta rented a room:

in the flat of a former cotton mill owner, who, thanks to the N.E.P., had suddenly found himself persona grata with the Soviet Government. He was offered the post of manager at his former mill, so that he could bring it back into working order. He was also permitted to keep the whole of the flat for himself and his family, though his living space was in excess of the norm.

The Nepmen were making an appearance. Liolia had a boyfriend who was affluent enough to give her presents of chocolate and silk stockings, luxuries that were still far too expensive for ordinary citizens to buy. Elisaveta discovered that he was:

engaged in speculation, an activity that mushroomed from the thin soil of private enterprise permitted under N.E.P. Men like Senya made quite a lot of money by buying goods in railway trucks, goods they had not even seen, and selling them at a profit to private traders. It was a mystery to me how this was done

47 Smolensk Market in Moscow, September 1921, after the legalization of private trade under the N.E.P.

Membership of the higher echelons of the Party brought many benefits, although many top leaders such as Lenin and Dzerzhinsky, head of the G.P.U., continued to lead austere lives. Officials were allowed to shop at special stores, where they could buy many things not yet available to the general public. Elisaveta observed that at the theatre:

The Soviet administrative elite were already conspicuous by the fresh look of their uniforms – admittedly still discreet in cut and trimmings – and by the obviously foreign provenance of their wives' frocks. Litvinov [Deputy Commissar for Foreign Affairs] and Ivy Lowe [his English wife], Lunacharsky [Commissar for Education] and his actress wife, would be frequently there, in the third or second row of the stalls, both wives wearing gorgeous evening dresses, such as an ordinary Soviet woman had never set her eyes upon in the shops.

With the end of the civil war had come a lessening of political repression. Although travel abroad was still difficult, it was now relatively easy to move around freely within the Soviet Union itself. Religion was still frowned upon as superstition but its practice was tolerated. Even the G.P.U., the successor to the Cheka, had acquired:

a milder image; the sentences they produced on political transgressors were more frequently "minus three" or "minus five" i.e. a prohibition to reside in three or five principal towns of the Soviet Union, rather than the highest measure of punishment in a Siberian labour camp.

The official attack on "bourgeois morality" and the old social conventions was welcomed by many young Russians; nude bathing, for example, had become a cult in Odessa even before the end of the civil war. Marriage and divorce were mere formalities. In 1921 Elisaveta Fen had contracted a marriage of convenience with a Latvian engineer, planning to use the Latvian citizenship she automatically acquired to emigrate from the Soviet Union. For personal reasons this plan fell through, and in 1925 she divorced the husband she had not seen for four years. It was very simple because:

the presence of the other partner was not required. You gave the clerk the name of the spouse who you wished to divorce and the date of your marriage; that was duly written down and you signed the statement which thus became a legal act of divorce. All you needed to do afterwards was to inform your former marriage partner.

The era of experimentation in the arts, that had begun in 1917, was not yet played out. Elisaveta attended a performance by an orchestra without a conductor, which was intended "to demonstrate that the collective principle could be applied in all spheres of human activity".

Elisaveta Fen was still far from reconciled to Soviet life. She sensed the Party's presence everywhere and could not rid herself of the feeling that she was always watched. Even at the Quaker Mission, where she worked for a while, rumours circulated that certain employees were stooges planted by the G.P.U. Moreover, she wrote poetry and stories on personal themes and had long hoped to earn her living as an author. In 1917 she had had a novel accepted by a publisher, only to see its chance of publication destroyed by the revolution. In 1924 Gosizdat, the state publishing house, rejected a batch of her love poems on the grounds that:

these poems are too pessimistic. Their tone is not consonant with the reality of Soviet life which should reflect a joyous, hopeful outlook and the Soviet woman's trust in her comrade, the man.

With "proletarian literature" all the rage, Elisaveta realized that her ambitions could never be fulfilled in Russia, and years of suppressed frustration came welling to the surface. Meeting foreigners she was envious of the way in which they:

could plan three, four, even six months ahead. . . . And here am I, unable for the last seven years to plan more than a few days ahead and always with an "if" in my mind – "if" nothing unforeseen happens in the interval, "if" the government does not suddenly publish a decree ordering all recent arrivals to leave Moscow, "if" some high-up at the G.P.U. does not suddenly decide to stop all exit visas from Russia.

In 1925 she applied for permission to visit England. Soviet contacts with the outside world were increasing at this time and, much to her astonishment, she was granted the right of a year's absence from Russia. She never settled there permanently again.

Lenin's Last Years (1921-1924)

At the close of the civil war the future of the Soviet Union was still far from certain. Lenin himself regarded the N.E.P. as a temporary expedient only, to tide over backward Russia until socialist revolutions should occur in the more advanced countries of Europe. He was likewise convinced that strict Party dictatorship must be tolerated as an interim measure until the Russian proletariat was mature enough to administer its own affairs. In 1921 he denounced the Communists of the Workers' Opposition, who wanted to move more rapidly towards "socialist democracy", as "infantile", ordered the suppression of the Kronstadt mutineers and wrote regretfully:

The workers would like to build a better apparatus for us, but they do not know how. . . . They have not yet developed the culture required for this. (Quoted in M. Lewin, *Lenin's Last Struggle,* Faber and Faber, 1969).

At that time, Lenin was still a vigorous man, whose ascendancy over the Communist Party was unquestioned. Preoccupied with day-to-day administration, he gave only limited consideration to the long-term implications of the "temporary" expedients he had been forced to adopt. On 26 May 1922, however, he suffered a severe stroke that paralysed the right side of his body and impaired his speech.

When he returned to public life in October of that year, there were clear indications that he was seriously worried about trends in Soviet political life. Previously, for example, the future status of the three Trans-Caucasian Republics had been seen as a minor issue. Then, on 12 December 1922, Lenin discovered that Ordzhonikidze, Moscow's representative in Georgia, had lost his temper and struck a Georgian Communist in the face. This was not, argued Lenin, just an ordinary clash of personalities, but a sign that the traditional arrogance of ethnic Russians towards the non-Russian nationalities had survived the revolution, and he wrote angrily to the Politburo:

From what I was told by Comrade Dzerzhinsky, who headed the commission sent by the Central Committee to investigate the Georgian incident, I could only derive the greatest apprehensions. If matters had come to such a pass that Ordzhonikidze could go to the extreme of applying physical violence, as Comrade Dzerzhinsky informed me, then you can imagine what a swamp we have gotten into. (Quoted in R. Payne, *The Life and Death of Lenin,* Allen, 1964)

It seemed, incredibly, as if some Soviet officials had inherited their attitudes directly from the Tsarist system, "only tarring them a little with the Soviet brush".

The day after this letter was written Lenin fell ill again; he was confined to his room in the

Kremlin by his doctors and forbidden to indulge in political activities or to receive any but personal visits. From the diaries kept by two of his secretaries, Lydia Fotieva and Marie Volodicheva, and by his sister Maria, it is clear that Lenin was desperate to maintain some sort of contact with the outside world. On 23 December he begged the doctors to allow him to dictate for five minutes a day, for "If I do not do it now, I may never be able to do it", and the doctors relented in the hope that it might relieve his mind. His secretaries and his wife, Nadezhda Krupskaya, smuggled documents into him and made notes of his conversations, which, on Lenin's orders, were kept secret from the rest of the Party. Of the five copies typed, one remained with him, three were given to Krupskaya, and one went into the secret file in his office. As his opportunities for comment on events were so limited, it is safe to assume that this "Testament" dealt with the issues that most preyed on Lenin's mind.

The Politburo gave to Stalin the task of ensuring that Lenin obeyed the doctors' instructions. It proved an unfortunate choice, for Stalin was determined to exploit his position to increase his influence in the Party at the expense of Trotsky, considered by many to be Lenin's natural successor. When, on 21 December, the Soviet leader dictated to Krupskaya a brief and friendly note addressed to Trotsky, Stalin regarded it as a serious blow to his plans and reacted violently. He berated Krupskaya on the telephone and upset her so much that she complained in indignation to Kamenev. When Lenin found out what had happened, he refused to see it as purely a personal issue and regarded it as a symptom of what was going wrong with the Party.

The Testament was dominated by Lenin's awareness of the dangers posed by Party dictatorship. The establishment of true socialism in Russia would only come about when the educational level of the workers and peasants had been raised, for:

There is only one thing we have left to do and that is to make our people so enlightened that they understand all the advantages of everybody participating in the work of the co-operatives, and organise this participation. Only that. There are now no other devices needed to advance socialism. (Quoted in Lewin)

Only then could coercion be abandoned and the workers' state become a reality. Social education was particularly needed in the rural areas, but Lenin realized that attempts to push the peasants too fast would be counter-productive, and he therefore suggested that urban workers organize themselves to go into the villages as political teachers. Meanwhile, as there was no real alternative to Party dictatorship in the short-term, the quality of the dictators was all-important; there should be none among them who loved power for its own sake, and it was on these grounds that Lenin found the behaviour of Stalin and Ordzhonikidze so appalling. In the pages of the Testament the characters of all the leading Communists were subjected to a ruthless analysis and their strengths and weaknesses revealed, but it was Stalin's character that most worried the Party leader and made his removal from the influential post of Party Secretary a priority.

The most scathing indictment, however, came on 23 January when Lenin dictated a letter to the Party Central Committee to be opened after his death; among further comments on leading Bolsheviks were the following:

Stalin is too coarse, and this fault, though tolerable in dealings among us communists, becomes unbearable in a General Secretary. Therefore I propose to the comrades to find some way of removing Stalin from his position and appointing somebody else who differs from Comrade Stalin in all respects – namely, more tolerant, more loyal, more polite and considerate to his comrades, less capricious etc.

Comrade Stalin . . . has concentrated in his own hands unbounded power and I am not sure whether he will always know how to use this power cautiously enough.

Two months later, on 7 March, Lenin

received a file on the "Georgian Affair", compiled by his devoted personal secretaries, and wrote immediately to the Georgian Communist leaders:

Esteemed Comrades!
    I am heart and soul behind you in this matter. Ordzhonikidze's brutalities and the connivance of Stalin and Dzerzhinsky have outraged me. I am now preparing notes and a speech.

Lydia Fotieva, meanwhile, begged Trotsky to support Lenin's stand:

His condition is getting worse every hour. You must not believe the reassuring statements of the doctors. He can speak now only with difficulty. . . . The Georgian question worries him terribly. He is afraid he will collapse before he can undertake anything. When he handed me this note he said: "Before it's too late . . . I am obliged to come out openly before the proper time."

Before the affair could develop further, Lenin suffered a third stroke that left him permanently speechless and ended his political life. On 21 January 1924 he died at the age of fifty-four. The struggles of his last years proved in vain and much of what Lenin feared came to pass. In May 1924 the Party Central Committee, dominated by Stalin's appointees, debated the Testament and concluded that Stalin's behaviour had improved so much since 1922 that there was now no need to obey Lenin's instructions. It was also decided to keep the Testament secret, and its contents were not revealed to the Party at large until 1956. Two years after Lenin's death the men he had denounced so vigorously occupied leading positions in Party and state – Ordzhonikidze as Chairman of the Central Committee and deputy head of government, Dzerzhinsky as Chairman of the National Economic Council and Stalin as Party Secretary, a position he exploited in order to impose a brutal dictatorship, not only over the Soviet people, but also over the Party itself, so that the last vestiges of the tradition of free debate were totally stifled.

It may be argued that Lenin's failure to curb Stalin was due to a combination of unfortunate circumstances. Many historians claim, however, that one-man dictatorship and the totalitarian state were inherent in the system Lenin himself created as a temporary expedient in the years after 1917. Perhaps the final word should rest with fellow-Communist, Rosa Luxemburg, who warned Lenin in 1918 that:

without general elections, without unrestricted freedom of the press and assembly, without a free struggle of opinion, life dies out of every public institution. . . . Public life gradually falls asleep and a few dozen party leaders of inexhaustible energy and boundless experience direct and rule. Among them, in reality, only a dozen outstanding leaders do the leading, and an elite of the working class is invited from time to time to meetings where they are to applaud the speeches of the leaders. (Quoted in R. Conquest, *Lenin,* Fontana, 1962)

NOTES ON RUSSIAN POLITICS

The Tsarist Autocracy

Before 1917 the Tsar (Emperor) of Russia wielded absolute power over the peoples of the Russian Empire, one of his many official titles being that of "Supreme Autocrat". After the 1905 revolution imperial power was limited by the establishment of the *State Duma*, a parliament or assembly elected on a narrow franchise of tax-payers and property-owners. All legislation had to pass through the Duma before it became law, and the Duma had the right to question, although not to appoint or dismiss, the Tsar's ministers. But even these modest powers were emasculated in 1907 when the Tsar's government tampered with the electoral law to ensure a safe conservative, monarchist majority. It was only in 1916, after Russia's disastrous performance in the first two years of the war, that the Duma became a centre of opposition to the Imperial Government.

The Political Parties

Centuries of autocratic rule, with strict censorship, tough restrictions on political activity and an intrusive secret police, had provided little opportunity for the development of conventional political parties. Instead, all this only encouraged the growth of conspiratorial revolutionary parties aiming at a complete overthrow of the existing political system and radical social change. It was in this climate that the *Socialist Revolutionary Party* and the *Russian Marxist Party* emerged.

While the former looked to the peasantry to provide the main revolutionary force, the Marxists believed that true revolution could take place only in an advanced industrial state with a numerous and politically-conscious working class (*proletariat*). Only in such circumstances, they argued, would the revolution culminate in *socialism*, in which the benefits of technology would be available to all, working people would freely run their own affairs, class distinctions disappear, and the now-superfluous state apparatus wither away. For *orthodox Marxists*, therefore, early twentieth-century Russia was far from ready for such a revolution. They accepted that the overthrow of the autocracy would have to be followed by a lengthy period of middle-class (bourgeois) government, during which time an industrial revolution and the operation of full civil liberties would enable the education of the proletariat to proceed to the point at which they could overthrow the bourgeois state and create socialism. Although acting in the name of the proletariat, the leaders of this movement, including the future Bolsheviks, Lenin, Trotsky, Kamenev, Zinoviev and Bukharin, came primarily from the small, educated professional class known as the "Intelligentsia".

In 1903 the Russian Marxists split into two factions. The *Mensheviks*, whose leaders included Martov and the future Prime Minister, Kerensky, adhered to orthodox Marxism. The *Bolsheviks*, under Lenin, planned to by-pass the Marxist theory of revolution in favour of an immediate socialist insurrection.

The partial lifting of restrictions on political activity after 1905 saw the emergence in Russia of non-revolutionary political parties on the Western-European model. The most important were the *Constitutional Democrats*, popularly known as the *Cadets*, who wanted to see the conversion of autocracy into a democratic parliamentary state. They drew the bulk of their support from enlightened landowners and middle-class professionals, many of whom had served their political apprenticeship in the *Zemstvos*, the elected local councils that had been the only form of representative government existing in Russia before 1905. The Cadets saw the Duma as the initial stage in the creation of a constitutional monarchy and, in their disillusionment, welcomed the February Revolution and formed the hub of the first Provisional Government. Their most prominent member, Paul Miliukov, took the post of Foreign Minister. Their influence never spread, however, beyond the numerically-small middle class, and during the course of 1917 Cadet ministers were gradually replaced by socialists, whose presence, it was hoped, would boost the government's flagging popularity. Miliukov, for example, was forced to resign as early as 10 May.

The Provisional Government and the Soviet

In the vacuum left by the abdication of Nicholas II, Duma deputies of the Cadet Party set up a temporary or *"provisional" government* to administer Russia until a directly-elected *Constituent Assembly* should decide on a permanent form of government. At the same time, however, *soviets* – councils elected by the rank and file in factories and regiments – sprang up in all Russian cities and military bases, the most influential of which was the *Petrograd Soviet*, to which delegates came from all over the country. Although their position was unofficial, it was to the soviets that the majority of workers and soldiers gave their allegiance, and the Provisional Government could do little without their consent. Perhaps the most important single thing to understand about Russia in 1917 is that whoever controlled the major soviets held the key to the control of the Russian cities.

In February 1917 Mensheviks dominated the Petrograd Soviet, but as popular support dropped away from the democratic socialists, Bolshevik influence grew until, in October, the Bolsheviks earned majorities in the critical Petrograd and Moscow Soviets. It was in the name of the soviets that the October Revolution was carried through, and the fiction, embodied in the name "Soviet Union", is maintained even today that Russia is run by freely-elected soviets. In fact, by the end of the civil war, soviets at all levels were under the close control of the Communist Party and were a means to manipulate rather than express the will of the Russian people.

The Organization of the Communist Party

In 1918 the Bolsheviks adopted the name *"Communist Party of the Soviet Union"*, by which it is known today. The leading Communists, by whom all important decisions were made, constituted the *Party Central Committee*, whose numbers fluctuated. However, within the Committee an elite emerged who ran the party from day to day; this was the *Politburo*. Under Lenin, the Central Committee met frequently and, until 1921, enjoyed a great measure of free discussion. Under Stalin, however, the Committee was consulted less often, its membership was severely purged and all real decision-making was confined to a small Politburo of men on whose loyalty Stalin could rely absolutely.

As a symbol of their break with the past, Bolshevik ministers were called *"People's Commissars"*; Trotsky, for instance, was Commissar for War and Lenin Chairman of the Council of Commissars, a sort of Prime Minister. More familiar, however, were the *political commissars*, dispatched from Moscow to supervise the operation of the Party and the army in the provinces. Any officer whose loyalty was in doubt, for example, had his personal commissar, who would watch for any deviation in the officer's behaviour, a system that continues in the Soviet armed forces today.

The Civil War
After November 1917 the old Tsarist Empire fell apart. Many transitory governments established themselves, especially in the frontier regions; some aimed at establishing autonomy from Moscow; others hoped to create a base from which to expel the Bolsheviks from central Russia. The main White regimes were:

1. The Cossack Republics
Until the eighteenth century the Cossack horsemen of the Don and Kuban River regions had lived in independent communities, outside the jurisdiction of the Russian Empire, supporting themselves through a mixture of agriculture and military raids on their neighbours (the Cossack territories have been described as the Russian equivalent of the American Wild West). Brought under the control of the Tsarist state during the course of the eighteenth century, the Cossacks retained special privileges, among them the right to form their own exclusive regiments within the Russian army, and until 1917 they responded by being the Tsar's most loyal troops, often used for riot-control. When Cossack regiments refused to fire on the demonstrators in Petrograd in March 1917 it heralded the beginning of the end of the Tsarist autocracy.

In the anarchic conditions of late 1917 the Cossacks seized the opportunity to recreate their traditional autonomous communities, ruled by elected *atamans*. In 1918 they sheltered, somewhat reluctantly, Denikin's embryonic White army, and co-operated with him in driving the Bolsheviks out of the region in early 1919. Their commitment to the advance on Moscow, however, was lukewarm, and when Denikin began his retreat in the autumn, the Cossacks deserted him in the hope that their homeland might be spared Bolshevik occupation. This hope proved vain, and all distinctive Cossack institutions were abolished by the Soviet government in 1920.

2. The Volunteer Army
This was formed by anti-Bolshevik officers in early 1918 and commanded after March of that year by General Denikin, who used it as the nucleus of the force for the recapture of Moscow. Needing to recruit the bulk of his army from the local population of Cossacks and peasants, Denikin never won their unequivocal support, for he insisted that nothing less would do than the restoration of the frontiers of the old Russian Empire, and in the areas he occupied the landlords were reinstated. In June 1919 the White armies of the South occupied the Ukraine and in October they captured Orel, only two hundred miles from Moscow. Forced to retreat soon after, they were driven out of southern Russia in the spring of 1920, a detachment under General Wrangel holding out in the stronghold of the Crimea until November.

3. Kolchak's Siberian Dictatorship
In May 1918 battalions of Czech prisoners-of-war, released by the Russians for service with the Allies on the western front and on their way to Vladivostok, quarrelled with the Bolsheviks and seized control of the Trans-Siberian railway, whereon Bolshevik rule in Siberia collapsed. In the vacuum created, Socialist Revolutionaries set up a democratic regime at Samara, which failed to win local support and was ousted by a band of determined army officers under Kolchak, a former Admiral of the Black Sea fleet. Calling himself Supreme Ruler of Russia and establishing his headquarters at Omsk, Kolchak and his army almost reached the River Volga in the spring of 1919. Like Denikin's, however, Kolchak's conscripted army was never reliable and harsh government, reminiscent of the worst abuses of the Tsarist system, caused disaffection in the rear. Forced to retreat in increasing disorder from May 1919 onwards, he was abandoned by the Czechs, who handed him over to the Bolsheviks for execution at Irkutsk in January 1920.

4. Yudenitch
Yudenitch was a former Tsarist general who created an anti-Bolshevik army in independent Estonia and defeated the Red Army in the north-west in early October 1919. With the army scattered and the local Communist party in a panic, Petrograd itself might well have been captured had Trotsky not rallied the population to its defence.

Archangel
In August 1918 a force of six thousand British, five thousand Americans and two thousand French, Italians and Serbs landed at Archangel in the Arctic Circle to defend ammunition stores against a rumoured German encroachment. In a typically confused scenario, the local Communist party was mysteriously overthrown and a Socialist Revolutionary regime emerged under the veteran socialist, Chaikovsky. Like all other "democratic" governments of this period, the Archangel regime failed to win appreciable popular support and degenerated in time into a military dictatorship under the senior British officer. In line with their policy elsewhere, the Allied troops took little advantage of the military opportunities but left the initiative to the local people themselves. When this failed to materialize, the Allied commitment gradually weakened and the last commandant, the British General Miller, fled on board an ice-breaker in February 1920, leaving his erstwhile Russian allies to face the advancing Red Army.

DATE LIST

1917

March 8-11	Strikes and demonstrations in the working-class districts of Petrograd; increasing fraternization between troops and demonstrators. Beginning of "February Revolution".
March 12	Organization of Petrograd Soviet of Workers' and Soldiers' Deputies.
March 15	Formation of first Provisional Government. Nicholas II and conservative Duma members still hope that the monarchy might be saved by a voluntary limitation of its powers, but the Tsar's attempt to return to Petrograd is prevented by insurgent railway workers who halt his train at Pskov. He is forced to abdicate.
April 16	Lenin's arrival at the Finland Station.

April 20	Publication of Lenin's April Theses, calling for uncompromising struggle against the Provisional Government and an end to the war. This is to become the basis of the successful Bolshevik programme of 1917.
May 17	Trotsky's arrival in Russia.
May 18	Reorganization of the Provisional Government to include Mensheviks and Socialist Revolutionaries. Chernov becomes Minister of Agriculture.
July 2	Beginning of Russian summer offensive, which fails disastrously and hastens disintegration of army.
July 16-18	"July Days". Unsuccessful rising by pro-Bolshevik workers and sailors – against the advice of Lenin. Lenin flees to Finland. Bolshevik Party declared illegal.
July 21	Kerensky becomes Premier.
September 6	Kornilov, Commander-in-Chief of Russian army, begins march on Petrograd, aimed at crushing Soviet and restoring law and order.
September 10	Collapse of Kornilov movement when his Cossack troops refuse to follow him. Restrictions on Bolshevik Party lifted, so that they can aid in defeat of Kornilov.
October 6	Bolshevik majority in Petrograd Soviet; Trotsky elected President.
October 23	Bolshevik Central Committee votes for armed insurrection.
November 7	Overthrow of Provisional Government in Petrograd; flight of Kerensky.
November 8	Institution of Council of People's Commissars; decree nationalizing land; armistice request sent to Central Powers.
November 9	Kerensky raises Cossack troops at Front and begins advance on Petrograd; beginning of battle between Soviet and pro-Provisional Government troops in Moscow.
November 12	Fighting in suburbs of Petrograd between Cossacks and Red Guard.
November 14	Kerensky's second flight.
November 15	Bolsheviks win control of Moscow. General Alekseev arrives in Don territory to begin formation of Volunteer Army.
Nov 25-27	Elections to Constituent Assembly held.
December 2	Escape of the generals from Bykhov.
December 15	Armistice with Central Powers.
December 20	Foundation of Cheka – the All-Russian Commission for Combating Counter-revolution, Sabotage and Speculation.

1918

January 18	Opening of Constituent Assembly.
January 19	Dissolution of Constituent Assembly by armed Bolshevik sailors and soldiers.
February 20	Decree for formation of Red Army.
February 23	After acrimonious debate, Bolshevik Central Committee accepts Lenin's insistence that German peace terms must be accepted.
February 25	Occupation of Don region by Red Army; Volunteer Army forced to flee to Kuban region.
March 3	Peace of Brest-Litovsk signed.
March 8	Bolsheviks change their name to Communists.
March 12	Capital moves from Petrograd to Moscow.
March 13	Trotsky becomes War Commissar.
April 6	Japanese arrive in Siberia.

April 9	Transcaucasian states including Georgia declare their independence.
April 29	German occupation of Ukraine.
May 6-8	Combined action of German and Cossack forces drives Communists out of the Don territory.
May 25-28	Czech Legion occupies key towns along Trans-Siberian railway and deposes Communists.
June 8	Establishment of Socialist Revolutionary government in Samara.
July 16	Former Tsar Nicholas II and his family shot in Ekaterinburg.
August 2	Allied troops land in Archangel and anti-Bolshevik democratic government established.
August 30	Lenin seriously wounded in an assassination attempt in Moscow. Powers of the Cheka increased, marking the beginning of the "Red Terror", which lasted until 1921.
October 8	Death of General Alekseev, first commander of Volunteer Army.
November 18	Kolchak declares himself Supreme Ruler of Russia and sets up his headquarters in Omsk. Democratic regimes in Siberia and Samara suppressed and a dictatorship established.

1919

January 6-13	Unsuccessful rising in Berlin by Sparticists (German Communists).
March 2-7	First congress of Communist International (Comintern) in Moscow.
March 13	Kolchak begins advance towards River Volga.
March 21	Communist regime established in Hungary.
April 26	Kolchak's advance halted.
June 4	Peasant guerillas led by Makhno attack Red Army in Ukraine and hasten Red retreat; Denikin, now commander of White armies in South, begins capture of Ukraine and Don region.

48 European Russia during the Civil War, 1918-21.

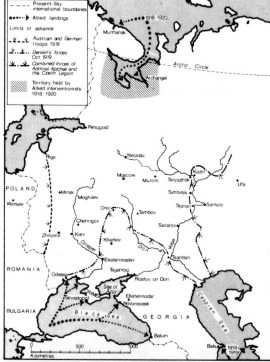

July 25	Red Army captures Chelyabinsk on Trans-Siberian railway; Kolchak's armies begin to disintegrate.
August 1	Fall of Hungarian Communist regime.
October 11	Yudenitch begins drive on Petrograd.
October 14	Denikin captures Orel, 200 miles from Moscow, the high point of his advance.
October 20	Orel recaptured by Red Army.
October 22	Workers of Petrograd drive Yudenitch back from suburbs.
November 14	Fall of Omsk, capital of Kolchak's Siberian regime, to the Red Army.
Dec. 12-16	Re-capture of Ukraine by Red Army.

1920

January 15	Czechs hand Kolchak over to Communists at Irkutsk.
February 7	Execution of Kolchak.
February 10	Beginning of organization of Red Army into labour battalions.
February 19	Capture of Archangel by Red Army; departure of Allied troops.
March 17	Capture of Novorosissk by Red Army.
April 14	Resignation of Denikin and appointment of General Wrangel as commander of White forces in south Russia.
May-Sept.	Russo-Polish War results in loss of sizeable territories on Russia's western frontier.
June 6	Wrangel leads a new White advance out of the Crimea.
November 2	Retreat of Wrangel's army back into the Crimea.
November 14	White armies evacuate the Crimea and White threat in South is eliminated.

1921

January	Beginning of serious peasant uprising against Soviet government in Tambov region.
February 27	Georgia invaded by Red Army and a Communist government established there.
March 1-7	Kronstadt rebellion. Sailors at the naval base, once the most loyal of Bolshevik supporters, demand the restoration of popular democracy in the form of freely elected Soviets and an uncensored press. They are brutally crushed by Red Army troops led by Trotsky.
March 8	Opening of Tenth Party Congress, which authorises the New Economic Policy and ban on factions.

1922

April	Stalin's appointment as General Secretary of the Russian Communist Party.
May 25	Lenin's first stroke.
November	Ordzhonikidze strikes the Georgian Communist, Kabanidze.
December 13	Lenin's second stroke.
Dec 23 – Jan 2	Major part of Lenin's Testament written.
December 30	Russia officially adopts name of Union of Soviet Socialist Republics (USSR) or Soviet Union.

1923

| March 10 | Another stroke ends Lenin's political life. |

1924

| January 21 | Death of Lenin. |
| May | Party Central Committee agrees to suppress Lenin's Testament. |

BOOK LIST

General Background
R. Charques, *The Twilight of Imperial Russia* (O.U.P., 1958)
H. Seton-Watson, *The Decline of Imperial Russia* (Methuen, 1952)
J.N. Westwood, *Endurance and Endeavour: Russian History 1812-1971* (O.U.P., 1973)
J.N. Westwood, *Russia, 1917-64* (Batsford, 1966)

Introductory Books on the Revolution and Civil War
A. Cash, *The Russian Revolution* (E. Benn, 1967)
D. Footman, *The Russian Revolutions* (Faber and Faber, 1962)
E.M. Halliday, *Russia in Revolution* (Cassell, 1967)
G. Katkov and H. Shukman, *Lenin's Path to Power: Bolshevism and the Destiny of Russia* (Library of the 20th Century, MacMillan/American Heritage, 1971)

More Detailed Books
E.H. Carr, *The Bolshevik Revolution 1917-1921*, 3 vols. (Pelican Books, 1966)
W.H. Chamberlin, *The Russian Revolution*, 2 vols. (The Universal Library, Grosset and Dunlap, New York, 1965) A classic.
G. Katkov, *Russia 1917* (Longmans, 1967)
M. Lewin, *Lenin's Last Struggle* (Faber and Faber, 1969)
R. Luckett, *The White Generals* (Longmans, 1971)

M. McCauley, ed., *The Russian Revolution and the Soviet State 1917-1921* (MacMillan, 1975)
A. Moorehead, *The Russian Revolution* (Panther Books, 1960)
L. Schapiro, *The Origins of the Communist Autocracy* (London, 1955) A very unfavourable view.

Biographies, Autobiographies and Memoirs
I. Deutscher, *The Prophet Armed* (O.U.P., 1954) First of a three-volume biography of Trotsky. A classic but difficult.
P. Fleming, *The Fate of Admiral Kolchak* (Hart-Davies, 1963)
R. Pethybridge, *Witnesses to the Russian Revolution* (Allen and Unwin, 1964)
J. Reed, *Ten Days that Shook the World* (Penguin, 1961)
V. Serge, *Memoirs of a Revolutionary* (O.U.P., 1963)
D. Shub, *Lenin* (Penguin, 1969)
Lenin for Beginners
Trotsky for Beginners (Writers and Readers Publishing Cooperative Ltd., 1978 and 1980) Left-wing publications, written in strip cartoon style with zest and a sense of humour. Quite unique!

Fiction
M. Sholokov, *And Quiet Flows the Don*
The Don Flows Home to the Sea (Random, 1965)
A. Solzhenitsyn, *Lenin in Zurich* (The Bodley Head Ltd, 1976)

INDEX

The figures in **bold type** refer to illustration numbers

Archangel, Socialist Revolutionary
government in 6, 8, 48-9, 69

Bolsheviks 3, 4-5, 8-9, 14-18 passim, 23-4, 27,
29-30, 32-3, 43-4, 68, 69
Britain:
and the Revolution 3, 45, 49-53
and the White regimes 27, 41, 45, 49-53,
69; **37**
attitude of British socialists to revolution 4,
55-6
Bryant, Louise 31-4
Bukharin, Nikolai 17

Cadet Party 7, 22-3, 68
Carmichael, Joel (historian) 20
Chaikovsky (Socialist Revolutionary) 23-4,
48-9, 69
Chamberlin, W.H. (historian) 4
Cheka 25, 30, 40-1, 54, 64
Chernov, Olga 37-41; **26**
Chernov, Victor 37-41 passim, **27**
Chkeidze (Georgian Menshevik) 61
Churchill, Winston 49
Civil War 3, 29-30, 69
Comintern 46
Commager, H.S. (historian) 45
Commissars: People's 30, 68
Political 9, 68
Communist Party, see Bolsheviks
Communist Russia:
cultural life in 64
education in 39
establishment of dictatorship in 3-4, 9, 57-9,
60-1, 65-7
life in 29-30, 35-6, 40-1, 62-5
role of Party in 60-1, 68-9
Constituent Assembly 4, 7, 38-9, 68; **29**
Cossacks 9, 28, 69; **18**
Czech Legion 39-40, 69

Denikin, General A.I. 9-10, 25-8 passim, 30; **38**
Duma 22-3, 68; **14**
Dzerzhinsky, Felix 64, 65-6 passim; **41**

Ekaterinburg 44

famine (1921-2) 30; **46**
February Revolution 3, 4, 7-9, 17, 18-20, 23,
29; **2**
Fen, Elisaveta 30, 62-5
First World War:
as a cause of revolution 22
policy of Provisional Government towards
7-8, 48
Fotieva, Lydia 66-7 passim
France:
and the revolution 3, 45, 69
aid to the Whites 27, 45
Francis, David 47-9

Georgia 61, 65-6 passim
Germany:
and the revolution 24; **17**

Communist revolutions in 7-8, 46
Goldman, Emma 56-9; **43**
Gorky, Maxim 8
G.P.U., see Cheka
Green Guards 5-6, 52

Hodgson, J. (journalist) 9

Julian calendar 6
July Days 20, 70

Kamenev, Lev 19, 66
and October Revolution 8-9, 60
Kanatchikov, Semen 11-14
Kerensky, Alexander 8, 32-3; **22**
Kolchak, Siberian dictatorship of 30, 39-40,
41-2, 69; **32**
Kornilov, Lavr 9, 26
Korostovetz, Vladimir 21-5
Kronstadt naval base:
as a centre of Bolshevism 4, 8, 30, 34; **11**
rebellion in 59, 71; **45**
Krupskaya, Nadezhda 66
Krylenko, Nikolai 33

Lansbury, George 53-6; **40**
Lenin, Vladimir **12, 13, 25**
others' opinions of 22, 32, 37, 53
philosophy of 8-9, 46, 65
tactics of in 1917 4, 8-9, 19-20, 26
Testament of 65-7
Litvinov, Maxim 17, 64
Lukomsky, General Alexander 25-8, 61; **17**
Luxemburg, Rosa 67

Maisky, Ivan 8
Makhno, Nestor 6, 61; **4**
Martov, Julius 8, 18
Marxism, theory of 7-9, 12-3, 19-20, 68
McCullagh, Frank 41-4
Mensheviks:
and civil war 8, 21
and revolution 7-8, 18-21
origins of 68
Miliukov, Paul 23, 68
Morison, S.E. (historian) 45
Moscow 6
during the civil war 30, 35-7, 58
under N.E.P. 62-5; **47**

New Economic Policy 61, 62-5
Nicholas II, Tsar of Russia 12, 22-3

October Revolution 4, 20-1, 33-4; **13, 23**
Omsk, capital of Kolchak's Siberian regime 30,
41-2
Ordzhonikidze, Grigory 65-7 passim

peasantry:
and civil war 5-6, 24-5, 39, 43; **15**
and revolution 4, 37-8; **28**
Petrograd (St Petersburg) 6
in civil war 5, 30, 35, 37; **3**
in 1917 4, 31-4; **2, 20, 21**

in pre-revolutionary days 13, 14-7
Petrograd Soviet 7, 20-1, 29, 68
Pravda 18
proletariat, see working class
Provisional Government 4, 7-8, 32, 68
purges, of 1930s 18, 21

Ransome, Arthur 21, 30, 34-7
Red Army 4, 27, 29, 30, 43; **45**
Red Guard 4, 39; **12**
Robien, Louis de 45-6 passim
Russell, Bertrand 4, 46

Samara, Socialist Revolutionary government in
6, 8, 39-40, 69
Shlyapnikov, Alexander 14-8
on February Revolution 8
Siberia, in civil war 42-4, 45; **32**
Smolny 21, 32-3; **4**
Socialist Revolutionary Party:
and civil war 6, 38-41
and peasantry 4, 7, 37-8
philosophy of 7, 68
soviets:
definition of 68
in civil war 44
in Petrograd, see Petrograd Soviet
role in government 60-1, 68
Stalin, Josef 14, 21, 66-7, 68; **12, 13**
Sukhanov, Nikolai 17, 18-21

Tambov rising 30, 71
Trotsky, Leon 5, 8-9, 32-3, 36, 44, 46; **33**
Tsarist (Imperial) army, and the revolution 15,
25, 32; **2, 17**

United States of America:
and Russian Revolution 3, 47-9
and Whites 48-9, 69; **35, 36**

Vlasov, Andrei 61
Volunteer Army, see White armies in south

war Communism 5, 29-30; **24**
Whites 4-5, 9-10, 30, 61
armies in Siberia 41-3, 69; **31, 32**
armies in south 5-6, 9-10, 25-8, 50-3, 69; **6**
Williamson, H.N.H. 49-53
Winter Palace 33-4; **23**
Workers' Opposition 4, 17, 61
Wrangel, General Peter 28, 61, 69; **6**
working class:
during revolution and civil war 5, 7-8,
19-21, 60
in pre-revolutionary days 14-6; **7, 8, 10**
their place in Marxist theory 7, 19-21, 60

Yudenitch, General 5, 69

Zelnik, Reginald (historian) 11-2
Zinoviev, Grigory 35, 61
and October Revolution 8-9, 60